The Cinema of Robert Rodriguez

The Cinema of Robert Rodriguez

By Frederick Luis Aldama
Foreword by Charles Ramírez Berg

University of Texas Press ⟨⟩ Austin

Requests for permission to reproduce material from this work should be
sent to:

Permissions
University of Texas Press
P.O. Box 7819
Austin, TX 78713-7819
http://utpress.utexas.edu/index.php/rp-form

♾ The paper used in this book meets the minimum requirements of
ANSI/NISO Z39.48-1992 (R1997) (Permanence of Paper).

LIBRARY OF CONGRESS CATALOGING-IN-PUBLICATION DATA
Aldama, Frederick Luis, 1969–
   The cinema of Robert Rodriguez / by Frederick Luis Aldama ; foreword
by Charles Ramírez Berg. — First edition.
      pages   cm
   Includes bibliographical references and index.
   ISBN 978-0-292-76121-6 (cloth : alk. paper) —
   ISBN 978-0-292-76124-7 (pbk. : alk. paper)
1. Rodriguez, Robert, 1968— Criticism and interpretation.   I. Title.
PN1998.3.R633A64   2015
791.4302′33092—dc23

                                        2014007099

doi:10.7560/761216

FOR CORINA ISABEL VILLENA-ALDAMA . . .
whose smarts, derring-do, and rascally ways won the honorific title "Spy Kid" from Robert Rodriguez

Contents

A Teaser before the Show

*L*ONG BEFORE FREDERICK LUIS ALDAMA COULD HAVE
conceived of the resplendent journey he recounts in *The Cinema
of Robert Rodriguez*, in the summer of 1991 Robert set out to make a film he
didn't expect anyone to see—at least not on the U.S. side of the U.S./Mexico
border. The film was *El Mariachi*.

You will learn of other details and nuances as captured by the different angles
presented in Aldama's book, but for now let me offer a teaser—a trailer, if you
will—that provides a snapshot of Robert's vision, practice, and significance.

He made *El Mariachi* for $7,000 and hoped to sell it to the Spanish language
video market for $15,000. With that money he intended to make Part 2. Then
he'd repeat the process and finish the Mariachi trilogy. "Those three films," he
says now, "were going to be my film school, because the only way you learn to
make movies is to make movies."

But his plan failed because *El Mariachi* was too good. He took it to LA,
where he waited for a Spanish-language video company to call back. One day,
he decided to drop off a tape of his nine-minute student film, "Bedhead," and
a two-minute *trailer* for *El Mariachi*, at International Creative Management,
one of the world's largest talent agencies. He just walked in off the street and
handed the tape to the receptionist, so I imagine he got a variation of the standard "Don't call us, kid, we'll call you" line. ICM called him the next day.

They loved "Bedhead," and were really interested in that trailer. Was it for a
feature? Was it finished? Could they see it? He immediately delivered a feature-
length copy of *El Mariachi*. "Why didn't you just drop off the complete *El Mariachi* the first time?" I asked him later. "I wanted them to ask me to see it," he
said, "instead of me asking them." You see how that changes the dynamic of the
relationship, and how savvy this junior in the Department of Radio-Television-

Film at the University of Texas was—and still is today. ICM loved *El Mariachi*, signed Robert, and got him a contract with Columbia Studios.

Columbia's first notion was for Robert to remake it in English (eliminating those dreaded subtitles) with a star in the lead. But to get an idea of how the film would play, Columbia sent Robert and *El Mariachi* (with subtitles) on the festival circuit. Festival audiences ate it up—subtitles and all. It won Audience Awards at the Sundance and Deauville Film Festivals, and Columbia decided to release it theatrically just as Robert made it. Receiving glowing reviews by critics (two thumbs up from Gene Siskel and Roger Ebert) and aided by the entertaining appearances Robert made on the *Today Show* and *David Letterman*, the movie was a sleeper hit, and Robert's career was off and running.

To bring the movie's journey full circle, in December of 2012 *El Mariachi* was added to the National Film Registry of the Library of Congress as an American film that will be preserved because of its cultural, historical, and aesthetic importance. Looking back, *El Mariachi* was a landmark film for at least three reasons.

First, it was a milestone for Latinos in U.S. film. There had never been a prodigious Latino talent like Robert in the Hollywood system—someone who wrote, directed, coproduced, edited, recorded and edited the sound, edited the music, and acted as cinematographer and camera operator on his first film. This was an unprecedented and unexpected kind of Latino filmmaker, a Mexican American combination of Orson Welles and Steven Spielberg.

Moreover, we'd never seen a Latino action hero in a Hollywood-released film either. Robert had smuggled a Latino protagonist into a popular genre, something he'd repeat again in the *Spy Kids* franchise and then in the *Machete* movies. All of a sudden audiences were cheering for Mexican guitar players, rooting for a young brother and sister named Cortez, and following the exploits of their mysterious Uncle Machete.

Second, it was a milestone for independent filmmaking. Yes, there were other indie hits released around the same time—this was, after all, the time of breakthrough films by Spike Lee, Steven Soderbergh, Rick Linklater, and Quentin Tarantino. But none of them had as compelling a making-of story as *El Mariachi*—an against-all-odds tale of a Mexican American college kid who made a hit feature film for $7,000 during his summer vacation. Indeed, Robert's book-length diary of the making of the film, *Rebel Without a Crew*, became the manifesto of new indie filmmaking.

Third, it set the template for DIY digital filmmaking—a decade before digital filmmaking existed. The "Mariachi Aesthetic," the movie-making method Robert devised to make *El Mariachi*, was revolutionary. Strip the list of things you think you must have to make your film down to zero—because that laundry list is only preventing you from getting to the business of actually making

Robert Rodriguez's DIY *Mariachi Aesthetic in the making of*
El Mariachi *(1992).*

your movie. Instead, make a list of the resources you *do* have, then fashion a movie around them. (For *El Mariachi* it was an antique bathtub, a sleepy dog, a bus, two bars, a hotel, a borrowed Arriflex camera, and a cooperative, one-take turtle.) Don't ask for permission. Don't wait for more money. The lack of money is a blessing, because it forces you to be more creative, and creativity will improve your movie more than money ever will. Get off your butt and go make your damn movie.

Robert's DIY Mariachi Aesthetic was a direct challenge to Hollywood's established Rules for Filmmaking. With budgets skyrocketing and the dependence on special effects growing exponentially, studio moviemaking in the 1990s was essentially a warning to beginning filmmakers to stay away. "Don't try this at home," big-budget Hollywood movies said. "Leave filmmaking to highly trained professionals with piles of money." By ignoring the warning and making *El Mariachi* his way, Robert burned the rule book.

Robert broke into studio filmmaking by doing the impossible: he made a really good, entertaining movie, on his own, for less than 1/10,000 of the budget of *Batman Returns*, 1992's blockbuster hit. To put it another way, for the cost of *Batman Returns*, Robert could have made 10,000 *El Mariachis*—and had $10 million left over. Incredibly, the cinematic boy wonder from Texas beat Hollywood at its own game.

Robert's unique qualities as a filmmaker—his originality, inventiveness, and healthy skepticism—are perfectly captured by Aldama. Combining his customary insightful analysis and lively prose style, Aldama examines Robert's entire career (so far) and explains what appears to be a contradiction—that while Robert has grown as a filmmaker he has basically stayed the same. He's spending way more than $7,000 per picture, yet the Mariachi Aesthetic remains intact: the innovation of ideas as well as vitality of creation realized in his cinema of possibilities continue to trump concerns over exorbitant blockbuster budgets. It was putting innovation and creativity ahead of big-dollar budget preoccupations that allowed him to make a special effects–intensive film like *Spy Kids* look like a $100 million movie for ⅓ of that cost. As Aldama so eloquently shows, Robert's healthy questioning of how studio movies are made led him to become one of the great pioneers of the silver screen; his firsts are many, including being the first filmmaker to switch to digital and the first to use green screen in such a way as to create one of the most remarkable graphic novel adaptations—Frank Miller's *Sin City*.

As his former professor, I am happy to have been one of the people around when Robert launched his career with *El Mariachi*. And I am equally happy to see the publication of Aldama's book. In many ways Aldama represents that generation of scholar who is not only engaged and intrigued by Robert's films, but who also can write a full-length book on this abundant corpus: from his earliest (including those shorts made in high school) to his latest (*Machete Kills*). To do so, Aldama completely immerses himself in the world of Rodriguez to share its riches with readers of all kinds across the globe. Aldama delivers a book made with some of that Rodriguez DIY sensibility that is alive to the richness of his topic, alert to the surprises he discovers along the way, and able to bring it to life with ease and grace. *The Cinema of Robert Rodriguez* represents something wonderful and significant: a top Latino critic looking at a top Latino filmmaker.

Charles Ramírez Berg
University Distinguished Teaching Professor in the Department
of Radio-Television-Film at the University of Texas at Austin

Acknowledgments

*B*IG ABRAZOS TO SAMUEL SALDÍVAR AND CHRISTOPHER González — one-finger push-ups present no problem for these superheroes cut in the mold of Osiris Amanpour (*Machete*). This book would not exist if it were not for Robert Rodriguez. It would not exist if Charles Ramírez Berg (former professor of Rodriguez's at UT Austin) had not helped open lines of communication with Rodriguez. Ramírez Berg knew Rodriguez before the titanic splash of *El Mariachi* (1992). As his professor in UT Austin's Department of Radio-Television-Film, he knew him before Rodriguez would explode onto the world cinematic stage. How grateful am I to Ramírez Berg? While I'm happily satisfied with one child, Corina Isabel Villena-Aldama, I should adopt another just to name her Charlie. That's how grateful. I can say the same of author Alvaro Rodriguez, who has actively helped me to build bridges between the creative and the scholarly. And last but not least, I whole heartedly thank Robert Rodriguez's gracious and generous assistant, Glenda Delgado, who has been instrumental in smoothing lines of communication with Rodriguez, the busiest Latino on this planet — and seemingly any and all other parallel planetary systems.

The Cinema of Robert Rodriguez

Art and Industry: The Films of Robert Rodriguez

ROBERT RODRIGUEZ STANDS APART FROM ALL OTHERS as the most productive U.S. Latino filmmaker working today. With seventeen films made since his first breakout success *El Mariachi* in 1992, he has single-handedly (and I mean this literally given that he scripts, directs, shoots, edits, and scores nearly all his films) crossed U.S. Latino filmmaking over into twenty-first-century global cinema. (This number does not include the additional films in various stages of production during the writing of this book: *Fire and Ice* and *Sin City: A Dame to Kill For*. Nor does it include all the made-for-cable films Rodriguez was overseeing in the lead-up to his launch of El Rey Network with Comcast in 2014.)

With his constant flow of film releases it is not surprising that Rodriguez receives a lion's share of entertainment media coverage. The news of his fourteen-day-shoot, $7,000-budgeted *El Mariachi* and the blitz of buzz terms like *mariachi style* or *guerilla filmmaker* marked the beginning of an unceasing flow of media attention. It could only be thus as he would continue to make films through the new millennium, fine-tuning his creative, low-cost, efficient filmmaking approach all the while. While a near constant fixture in the mainstream media, the systematic scholarly study of Rodriguez's films is only just beginning. There has been a sprinkle of academic essays on his work, and only two book-length studies. With only three of his films released (*El Mariachi*, *Desperado*, and *From Dusk till Dawn*), in 1998 Barbara J. Marvis recognized that he should be the subject of a biographical book series for children on significant Latino figures; aimed at teaching primary-school children, Marvis's *Robert Rodriguez* is a very thin book on his life and those above-mentioned films. With Europeans having taken a great interest in Rodriguez, it is not surprising that the first book-length scholarly study of his films should appear in Italy—a big producer of westerns (spaghetti) and horror (zombie) films; in several of Rodriguez's films one can see much inspiration coming from directors such as Sergio Leone and Dario Argento, among others. In 2009 Fabio Migneco published *Il cinema di Robert Rodriguez*. However, written in Italian and as of yet untranslated, Migneco's book remains limited to a European publishing market.

The writing of this book, along with the publishing of several edited collections on Rodriguez's work, marks a shift in the tide. In 2012 Zachary Ingle brought together under one cover many of the substantive interviews conducted with Rodriguez since 1993; many of the interviews appearing in important journals such as *Sight & Sound* offer tremendous insight into Rodriguez's filmmaking approach generally and techniques specifically. Christopher González brings together important scholarly essays in a special issue of the journal *Post Script: Essays in Film and the Humanities*. To further solidify Rodriguez's films as a subject of scholarly study, in *Critical Approaches to the Films of Robert Rodriguez* (forthcoming), I bring together a series of scholarly essays in a single volume that variously consider matters of content (questions of representation), matters of form (such as his genre cross-pollination), and matters of affect and cognition (how the films trigger thoughts and feelings). Finally, given Rodriguez's central place in the making of Latino pop culture, his work is given a prominent place in my edited volume *Latinos and Narrative Media: Participation and Portrayal*.

In this single-director focused book I attend to all of Rodriguez's (feature) films to enrich our understanding of just how Rodriguez's films are made (nuts and bolts) and consumed (perception, thought, feeling). Along with the scholarly work mentioned above, the aim of this book is to turn ever more the spotlight onto Rodriguez's films as an area that necessitates serious scholarly study. This is just the beginning, of course.

I should briefly add this. It is certainly not that someone such as Rodriguez requires people like myself to exist—in any real material sense of that term. As I mentioned, the media has exercised its interpretive muscle many a time with the release of each of his films. More often than not, the media spins opinion (individual taste) or additional publicity in the guise of critical interpretation; it can often function as an appendage to publicity. Scholarly interpretation, however, has the opportunity to go more deeply into subjects of inquiry. In this interpretation of Rodriguez's films as cultural phenomena (as products of his reasoning, emotion, and imagination) that he spins out of himself, I begin to assign meaning to creations—his aesthetic products—and to assess their value and importance to humankind. In this fundamental and foundational sense of *knowledge making*, then, it does matter that we focus our sights on Robert Rodriguez—one of the most significant directors of the twenty-first century.

That Rodriguez was born in 1968 is significant. He would grow up during a sociohistorical epoch when he could realize his dream to become a filmmaker. I mean by this that Rodriguez was definitely born at the right time. Already in his early teens, technologies for recording and watching film were becoming more and more cost accessible to the average middle-class family. By his thirties, filmmaking technology was moving away from expensive, cumbersome cameras and editing machines to lightweight digital cameras and highly sophisticated postproduction computer graphic editing software.

Let's compare this briefly to the 1950s—not to mention those even more monolithic, hugely proportioned cameras of Eisenstein's day. Already in the 1950s directors needed elaborate and cumbersome structures to hold and move their film cameras; to generate the necessary wattage, projectors were also enormous. With big machines comes big cost. Once a script was ready, it might take years to secure enough financing to shoot a film. Everything about the technical apparatus involved in its making and projecting was costly and labor intensive. Indeed, making films independent of the studios was cost prohibitive; and what is today rather simple to accomplish with two shots to make a simple 180-degree dialogue sequence was then very labor intensive, involving moving heavy lighting equipment, not to mention behemoth-sized cameras. It was so cumbersome that often dialogue sequences would simply have the camera shoot two actors sitting in a row on a couch talking—that way, they would both be included in the shot. This is why, after years of trying to make a go of it in the film business (he even used his own house and actor friends to try to keep costs down) a director like Elia Kazan actually got out of the business. He would go on to direct his creativity into the singular pursuit of writing novels—best sellers at that.

I should mention briefly a director who chose not to let the burdens of costly and laborious technology get the better of him, Ed Wood. During this same epoch Wood decided to script, direct, edit, act in, and produce low-budget, quickly shot horror, sci-fi, and sexploitation films such as *Glen or Glenda* (1953), *Bride of the Monster* (1955), and *Plan 9 from Outer Space* (1959). With few retakes and lots of shortcuts, he cranked out low–production value films simply to entertain. Yet, Wood still existed in a time and place. His films didn't have an audience. Despondent and dismayed with the system, he too turned away from film (only later in his life would he try his hand at making porno films) to write novels—pulp and horror in his case. If Kazan's (or Wood's) so-called accident of birth had been 1968 and they had grown up as teens and then adults to have the same access to filmmaking technologies as Rodriguez had, my guess is that Kazan (and Wood) would have continued making films.

Rodriguez was born in the late 1960s and did grow up during a time when filmmaking technology was becoming more accessible—and to a Latino. (Later, I'll discuss at length this aspect of his coming-of-age as a Latino during a time of the huge Latino demographic explosion and the significance of this.) Lightweight VHS cameras and home VCRs allowed Rodriguez to shoot, then edit dozens of shorts (using his friends and siblings as actors) as a teen and young adult. VHS technology also allowed him to watch all sorts of movies—and study the craft of those directors who caught his eye such as John Carpenter. That is, Rodriguez's coming of age as a filmmaker during this period offered him the possibility of honing his craft from shooting to editing to sound designing in a completely self-sufficient way. Of course, while he cut his teeth as a filmmaker on VHS technology, it had its limits. He knew that for his self-education to continue, he would have to have access to the costlier technology of the 16mm camera and its film stock. Fortunately, this was a time, too, when one could realize filmmaker ambitions in certain public university settings, one of which happened to be in the Department of Radio-Television-Film at the University of Texas at Austin.

Rodriguez is a filmmaker very much shaped by the circumstances of the era in which he came of age as a filmmaker; of course, as the technology progressed, so too did Rodriguez. With *Desperado* (1995) he learned how to use a Steadicam; with *Spy Kids 2* (2002) and *Once Upon a Time in Mexico* (2003) he taught himself HD film techniques; with *Sin City* (2005) he honed his CGI, animatic, and green screen skills. With *Spy Kids 3* (2003) he resurrected 3-D filmmaking; with *Spy Kids 4D* (2011) he added a fourth dimension—smell. He did so all in the *actual making* of his films. His home-school approach to filmmaking continues and allows him, unlike his ingenious and creative predecessor Kazan, to continue to make films (and make a living making these films) outside the studio system. With the exception of a few films like *The Faculty* (1998), where he was brought on by the Weinstein brothers (Bob and Harvey) to give cinematographic flesh to an already fully conceived script (Kevin Williamson's rewrite of an original script by David Wechter and Bruce Kimmel), in nearly all of Rodriguez's films, he maintains total control over his products. (Even with this more predetermined film, Rodriguez managed to make it his own—sometimes in very subtle ways. According to Alvaro Rodriguez, Robert Rodriguez brought sound bites into the script from his high school days and included a yellow jacket, or wasp, as the high school's mascot—the same mascot as his alma mater's, St. Anthony's High School Seminary in San Antonio; and he uses St. Anthony's high school's colors, maroon and gold, as the high school colors in *The Faculty*.) He is screenwriter, director, cinematographer, producer, sound engineer, production designer, visual and sound-effects editor, and music-score composer. He is adept at traditional and digital filmmaking, computer graphics effects, and digital editing. This has allowed for the growing of his creative personality—his artistry.

The moment he would face any obstacle to the realization of his creativity, he would find a solution. On one occasion, this even meant rejecting the mandates of the Directors Guild of America. I'll speak more to this later, but they denied him the possibility of crediting Frank Miller as codirector of *Sin City*. He pulled out of the guild knowing that this would also lose him paychecks from Hollywood studios attached to the DGA. (See Daniel Engber's "Why Not Quit the Directors Guild? What Robert Rodriguez Can and Can't Do.") He inserted the codirecting credit and made the film with Miller—and has made many films outside the studio system ever since.

LATINO AUTEUR, AND THEN SOME

Does this total control over the creation of his films make Rodriguez an auteur?

When I hear *auteur* I think of the French *Cahiers du cinema* (1951–present), which was cofounded by the film theorist André Bazin and included critics-turned-directors such as François Truffaut, Jean-Luc Godard, Éric Rohmer, and Claude Chabrol, among others. I think of the film critic Andrew Sarris's identifying of an *auteur*'s imprint on a given film in contradistinction to the churning out of film after film as per the factory approach to filmmaking in the Hollywood studio system. I think of the experimentalism of the French New Wave (or *La Nouvelle Vague*). I think of the Cinémathèque Française—and art-house exhibition venues more generally. I think of François Truffaut's more serious brand of youthful existentialism in *Les Quatre Cents Coups* (1959) and of the metafictional variety seen in Jean-Luc Godard's *À bout de souffle* (1960), where he breaks the so-called fourth wall with his use of out-of-sequence edits and the direct address (characters talking directly to the camera).

When I think of such seemingly precious films, I don't think of Rodriguez. Yet, Rodriguez also seeks total control over his product. In *Rebel Without a Crew* he remarks: "Although filmmaking is known as a collaborative art, it doesn't have to be. There's certainly no rule that says it has to be" (201). And his very varied films have a distinctive stamp: casting all sorts (Latino or otherwise) with and against type; quick rhythmic pacing; cross-pollination of genres; varied film texture from high-gloss Hollywood to grindhouse-flick scratched effects. Rodriguez's films, above and beyond all else, seek to entertain. Even his arguably most sociopolitical film, *Machete*, with its heavy nod toward Arizona's anti-immigration policies and brutalities met by those crossing the U.S./Mexico border, aims to ultimately *entertain*.

To put it simply, when watching a Rodriguez film, one imagines him serious about his work, but also smiling (even if with the occasional tongue in cheek), and with a Truffaut and a Godard, one imagines only straight-faced seriousness. They all seek total control over their products, but their ambitions and world-views as filmmakers couldn't be more different.

We might consider Rodriguez's brand of auteurism as his practice of a do-it-yourself sensibility *and then some*. As he mentions in his "Ten Minute Film School" series (often included as part of the features on the film DVDs), he usually learns to a great degree of technical proficiency the different elements that make up the film, for efficiency's sake and therefore also for cost's sake. Rather than send the film out postproduction for a composer to come up with a sound design that takes up much time and money, he would rather learn (as he has) how to compose on the spot.

The same can be said of his learning all the other elements of the filmmaking process. So while his orchestration of all the elements is total, this is driven less by the ambition to give the product a distinctive authorial stamp than by time and money. I would argue that this is why his films do end up having a distinc-tive Rodriguez quality as mentioned above, but also why they aim to divert in a nonhighbrow, pop culture manner. That is, with Rodriguez we have an auteur in the sense of a creative mind who has a *total vision* and *total control* of the making of the whole *with a specific audience in mind*—an audience that seeks above all else to be entertained. He pushes the envelope on cinematic language, creating the seemingly unimaginable in films like *Sin City*, but in ways that still aim, as the sine qua non, to entertain.

Rodriguez cross-pollinates genres and upturns themes and character types to at once entertain *and* self-reflexively open eyes to film conventions used to represent the reorganizing of a reality lived in and experienced by Latinos and all others—transmogrifying borderland vamps included. His films tell stories of all sorts—and in all variety of form and style: from the U.S./Mexican border-land Western as seen with the so-called Mariachi trilogy (*El Mariachi*, *Des-perado*, and *Once Upon a Time in Mexico*); to his mash-up road-movie/noir/goth/horror with *From Dusk till Dawn* (1996); to teen high school/sci-fi/hor-ror with *The Faculty*; to his wildly imaginative kid flicks with his *Spy Kids* fran-chise, *Shorts* (2009), and *The Adventures of Sharkboy and Lavagirl* (2005); to his noir and Catholic taboo crossing comic-book adaptation with *Sin City* (with Frank Miller); and to his recent B-genre/grindhouse/Mexploitation social-realist/parodic send-ups with *Planet Terror*, *Machete*, and *Machete Kills*. In each of his films, Rodriguez asks his audience to apprehend the whole—that is, how the parts cohere into an audiovisual organic whole in its relationship with the viewer. The blood and gore of *Planet Terror* (2007), for instance, might not appeal to all audiences, but its parts do pull together and cohere as a whole; its total effect in form and content triggers the right *oohs* and *ahs* in its audience.

This is why each of Rodriguez's technical choices—from shooting to scoring and editing—does make a difference. If at a given moment one ingredient doesn't cohere, the film might not cohere as an organic, unified whole with a unified affect. And, the less a director like Rodriguez has control over these elements, the more likely they will not cohere. While this can be the result of a director's choices, it is often external producer pressures (Kazan's great and totally justified gripe) or a lack of correspondence between one of the many mini-creators usually involved in the filmmaking process like the sound designer or editor.

LATINO PRINCIPIA AESTETICA

This MC (emcee, or master of ceremonies) controlling impulse in Rodriguez is the expression of a creative mind that seeks to control how the elements make up the whole as an aesthetic object. Of course, while we have come to know him as the "rebel without a crew" and know that he's very much a hands-on director (we see this even on a film that he didn't direct but only produced like *Predators*), he's a director also very much tuned in to the creativity of the many minds that surround him. His realization of his vision into an aesthetic object is very much the result of the many mini–creative minds working together.

As I discuss elsewhere, the aesthetic is a relation. That is, it is not found in the film—the object per se. Nor is it to be found in the subject—the filmgoer. It is in the relationship that Rodriguez creates between the film and the filmgoer. In Bertolt Brecht's small treatise on what he called his "epic theater" he discusses this need for a distance between the object and the subject in order to establish an aesthetic relation: if the relation is too proximate or too close, then no aesthetic relation is established. Later in this book I ask if in *Spy Kids 3* the video-game aesthetic is capacious enough for it to translate into film. Perhaps its structure disallows the kind of complex aesthetic relation possible in film.

Rodriguez organizes all the visual and auditory ingredients of any given film in such a way and with such a deliberate purpose so as to create a relationship between it and the filmgoer; to create a film that in its relationship to the viewer will trigger certain thoughts and feelings. This can and does happen with the way he chooses to use the visuals (lens, angles, lighting) and the auditory elements (sounds inside or outside the storyworld) to synch up in ways that create a series of *peak emotions*; it is the way he uses the elements in their totality to create a certain *mood* that lasts long after the experience of each individual peak emotion. That is, Rodriguez carefully constructs films that create a specific relationship with the filmgoer.

Of course, not all filmgoers will experience his films in the ways that he intends; while my basic emotions such as fear and happiness are at base the same as all others on the planet (our shared evolution ensures this), the particular experiences I have had and the way that I, as a unique personality, have processed these as I've grown in the world will necessarily shade differently the way I might experience the emotion of fear when seeing Salma Hayek transmogrify into a vampire in *From Dusk till Dawn* or Bruce Willis morph into a pustule-ridden monster in *Planet Terror*. This doesn't, however, take away from the fact that Rodriguez has created these objects with the aim of triggering specific emotions, thoughts, and worldviews in his audience. Indeed, a careful study of his films can determine what each film aims to do in relation to its, say, ideal audience, even if the flesh-and-blood audience doesn't actually react in these ways.

In each of his films, Rodriguez creates a specific relationship to an ideal audience. *Spy Kids* exists in relationship with an ideal audience that differs radically from the ideal audience of *Planet Terror*, for instance. With this audience in mind, he seeks as his goal to transform the story conceived in his mind into a film. In other words, his act of making real the fictional film as an object for filmgoers to respond to is the result of *intention*. As we know from interviews and his book *Rebel Without a Crew*, Rodriguez often has the idea first (sometimes years before actually making it into a film) that he then works on in his mind before taking the time and effort to make material. In *Rebel*, for instance, he discusses how after having the idea — guitar player turned *pistolero* — he then creates the whole film in his head before shooting. (He shares this same visual skill with the likes of Hitchcock and Welles.) Even before he shoots, he imagines the shots cut and edited into the final film complete with actors and angles. This way he can also be more precise about what has to be shot — and what he can do without.

For instance, in 1995 when Rodriguez made his short film "The Misbehavers" (as part of the anthology *Four Rooms*), he had an image of two kids dressed up in formal, James Bond–like outfits. The image as such is just an image. It just happens that it's an image that obsessed Rodriguez for a number of years. He wanted to turn this image into a story. During this period Rodriguez's imagination begins to give shape to this idea; he works upon this prime matter in his mind, and then he takes this product of his imagination and gives it shape as a story in his mind — kids who are spies who save their parents and the world — that then, through much labor, gives formal expression to this in the shape of a film called *Spy Kids*.

In his *Nicomachean Ethics* Aristotle discusses how human activity is purposeful. The carpenter has an idea of a table; then he uses the available materials and tools along with whatever skills to turn this idea into an object that corresponds to this idea. We can say the same of Rodriguez, who, like any other filmmaker, has a series of ideas, concepts, images (a whole series of mental representations) that he uses his skill as a filmmaker to objectify in the form of an audiovisual storytelling product we call film with the purpose of triggering an attitude, behavior, and emotional and intellectual reaction on the filmgoer. The technical elements that Rodriguez chooses to use in any given film shape the content of the story. In this sense, the story proper is the prime matter—understood as transformed matter, first worked upon already by Rodriguez's imagination before he even sets a pen to paper to sketch out a screenplay, storyboard, or even comic book. (See the comic he created, which appeared along with his script for "The Misbehavers" in *Four Rooms: Four Friends Telling Four Stories Making One Film.*) Once he has his story in mind and on paper, it undergoes a series of transformations with Rodriguez's choice of angle of a camera, lighting, music score, actor, and location. In what has been, say, made material as a film we find a correlation between not only the purpose of Rodriguez, but also the accomplishment of him as a filmmaker with a certain purpose to create a specific relation between the film and the viewer.

But Rodriguez's films are this and more. They are not simply a mirror reflection of reality nor a copy or an imitation of anything in the real world. His films are fictional and therefore they are *only* and *exclusively* an invented reality. Indeed, in a world made of law-like processes and structures stretching from the inorganic, through the organic, to the social, Rodriguez creates his fictional films by using his knowledge of causality (A to B to C) and his capacity for imagining different effects or causal results by mentally projecting outcomes (if A, then C, then possibly B). Rodriguez exercises such universal causal and counterfactual capacities specifically in relation to the making of fictional films. To do so, he exercises his emotive and cognitive systems; they allow him to ponder, assess, and modify his decisions and actions when making a film. Working together, his emotion and reason systems allow him to exercise this capacity for causal and counterfactual (and probabilistic) thinking or mapping of his physical (objects and functions) and social (people and institutions) worlds. He then works to accomplish the goal of making real his idea turned story turned film and is rewarded; we all experience the neurochemical release of oxytocin and dopamine—the feel-good brain drugs—when we accomplish tasks. He gets a kickback in the making of his films—and so too do his filmgoers experience a kickback if they step into the shoes of his ideal audience.

Rodriguez exercises his mental and physical capacities to, in effect, draw from recognizable social relations (people interactions) and physical objects (organic and inorganic) and then reorganize these into new aesthetic *artifacts* in the world; he creates films whereby the filmgoer recognizes people as people, monsters as monsters, cars as cars, explosions as explosions, but in the last instance as *constructs* that exist solely for the sake of entertainment—and aesthetic contemplation and satisfaction.

This is to say, the moment Rodriguez introduces any of the building blocks of reality into his films, these building blocks take on a different ontological status. They are no longer *real*—they are fictionalized. Put simply, Rodriguez is not asking that his audiences come to watch his films to learn something about the world; this might happen, but it is an ancillary function. We don't go to see *Machete* (2010) to learn about the anti-immigration policy or to see *Spy Kids* to learn how to raise a family. Yes, we might learn something about both, but this is not the main purpose. Such elements are there in the films just mentioned, but as appeals to the filmgoer to experience the film as organic wholes; that is, to partake or share with Rodriguez the emotions and attitude he wishes to convey and wishes the filmgoer to receive and therefore to behave accordingly.

Rodriguez's creating of films aims to make aesthetic objects whereby all ingredients (form and content) form an organic whole; a whole that we as the subject (filmgoer) are meant to apprehend as something shaped for contemplation—as well as to, in a way, educate the senses—especially the main aesthetic senses: visual and aural. Moreover, we see in Rodriguez a director whose control over all the ingredients is very much a trial and error in this aesthetic activity: determining the aesthetic means and their adequacy to his aesthetic goals, both seen from the viewpoint of the creation of the *new* aesthetic object as an organic whole.

In making *new*, Rodriguez revitalizes the filmgoers' sense of the world and all that is in it by making a new aesthetic relation between the film and filmgoer. The Russian formalists (Viktor Shklovsky in particular) identified this making *new* as the device or mechanism of *enstrangement*. It is through his use of film ingredients that he gives new shape to that which we have habituated ourselves to also in terms of film formula and convention: the noir, *narcotraficante*, sci-fi, Western, and spy genres, for instance. The genre of the noir hasn't changed much in terms of content (shadows cast from blinds, dames in distress, nihilistic loners against the world) in his and Miller's film *Sin City*, but the way they give shape to this content by this mechanism of *enstrangement* renews our apprehension of this genre.

Indeed, in all of Rodriguez's films we see his breaking the unaesthetic relation of habituation with the object by turning this object into something vital and new. This allows him to breach all kinds of social rules and norms and values (and physical laws) in *Machete* and *Planet Terror*, for instance. But it also allows him more generally to reconsider, as Sue J. Kim remarks, such issues as what does "a hero or villain look like? Who can be a film producer or director (i.e., who can tell the stories)? What even constitutes a movie?" (202). In other words, Rodriguez's films can open our perception, thought, feeling to what *is* possible and not to what *was* possible.

RECIPES

The film recipe (or architect's blueprint, as I identify it elsewhere) encompasses all the ingredients available to Rodriguez in the making of his films, including lens type, camera placement, lighting, scene composition, actor/character look and type, costuming, motion, and editing. All his films are made according to recipes. I use recipe in the spirit of his interest in sharing recipes such as in his short cooking school lesson on how to make Puerco Pibil as part of the DVD features included in *Once Upon a Time in Mexico*. His films are made up of specific ingredients from technical devices and structures used for plots, events, and character dialogue and action. His various filmic recipes also convey the sense that all these elements that make up any given film are not the *result* of a single entity.

While Rodriguez certainly exerts a great degree of willfulness over the ingredients used and how they integrate to make a whole, the total product is still the result of many skilled people working on and off (postproduction) his sets: from light engineers to costumers, special effects programmers, to set designers, and actors. A case in point: as Rodriguez's technical range and sophistication expand, so too does the list of credits that follow the ends of his films. Indeed, films that generally suffer from a diminished willfulness (or what I call elsewhere a "will to style") usually fail to cohere and the final product falls flat. Of course, too great a willfulness can result in the sense of a director's not incorporating the ideas of the many minds involved in the making of a film, and this can also lead to a flawed product. (For examples of the will to style and the making of flawed film products, see my *Mex-Ciné*.)

Rodriguez exerts a great degree of willfulness in his use of his imagination and technique, not just behind the camera, but also in the editing, scoring, and casting of his films. After the directing (framing, lensing, shooting) editing is arguably the most important ingredient to give a film its unique taste, say. On a basic level, editing can create all sorts of harmonious and discordant emotions and thoughts. We don't need to know Eisenstein's theory of montage to know that the juxtaposition of discordant images in the flow of the film creates odd, disparate emotions and thoughts; with our synthetic act of making sense of these disparate images we experience discomforting emotions and even a unique new way of seeing things. Nor do we need to know the theories of another Russian director, Vsevolod Pudovkin, to understand the significance of editing in terms of focusing the attention of the filmgoer and that bad editing can make a mess of how we apprehend, make sense, and experience emotion during the viewing of a film. As Rodriguez knows well and speaks to in his various "Ten Minute Film School" episodes, careful editing is not simply splicing together shots, but rather a tool the director uses to guide the emotions and meaning-making processes of the filmgoer.

Indeed, Colin McGinn remarks, "movie art is largely the science of converting feeling into action, making movement the bearer of emotion" (127). It is for this reason that Rodriguez has fought long and hard to maintain control over this very important shaping device, one that ultimately has the last say on how his films convert feeling into action and make movement the bearer of emotion. Even the movement created by sharply juxtaposing images—the montage in *Planet Terror*, and *Machete*, for instance—is usually not so radical as to be perceptually and psychologically intolerable and incomprehensible. If there were no sense to the montage, then we would simply lose interest; we would go elsewhere to fulfill our perceptual and psychological needs.

Rodriguez, with a nonprofessional background in music, but knowing how to play the guitar (and having learned to play the saxophone as a child), also insists on scoring his films. While he knows how to read music, he also learned how to use computer software to compose for a variety of instruments. He then sends this composition out to be rerecorded by professionals such as the Austin Philharmonic, Tito & Tarantula, and his band Chingon. (Rodriguez not only teaches himself how to use this technology as it advances, but also actively learns by asking questions of the music composer veterans like Danny Elfman.) Indeed, while most films are made, then sent out to composers to score, Rodriguez begins scoring his films as early as possible—even, on occasion, doing this work while writing the script. He considers it a crucial shaping ingredient that should not be left as an afterthought. Often, he walks around the set with a guitar—making up tunes that might not even be for the film he's working on, but one still to be made; it was on the set of *Desperado* that he first came up with the sound motifs and themes that he would use years later in the making of *Once Upon a Time in Mexico*. Also acutely aware of the strategic use of silence, he carefully orchestrates its distribution in the sound design as a way of generating the different emotions experienced in a film.

There is the equally important ingredient of casting that he maintains control over. Just as he often scores as he writes the script, he also often casts as he imagines the story. He has in mind already, while working out the story, which actor will play which character; by the time the screenplay is finished, often he's already got a cast credit laid out. That is, he imagines and then writes with individual actors in mind and therefore with their strengths and weaknesses in mind too. By controlling this ingredient, Rodriguez also controls the final product: casting actors who are believable and move the story forward. And once on set, he can continue to grow organically the script; he modifies—and in some cases even finishes—the script during the shoot, building in obstacles and conflicts that build on the strengths of the actors. So while a roughed-out script is ready to go before the shoot, there is writing and rewriting during the production. This becomes the organically grown template for the actors and crew on the set to understand what Rodriguez is shooting, cutting, and finalizing in his head.

IMPLIED DIRECTOR "RODRIGUEZ"

As chef in the kitchen, Rodriguez of course uses many more ingredients than the few key spices just mentioned. The different mixtures make for different results, of course. As each film comes out of the oven, it has a unique texture and taste. Individually and collectively, the films generate in the viewer a sense of the maker.

We can identify this entity as the chef—or as I've done above, the grand conductor, or master of ceremonies of film devices. Another way to consider this is that in each film, the ingredients used and their unique combination add up to our sense of the *implied* director's worldview. In *Narration in the Fiction Film* David Bordwell declares that we are well served by talking about film as "the organization of a set of cues for the construction of a story. To this we might add the useful concept of the implied director or implied creator" (62). This concept of the implied director or implied creator is useful. This is not the same as the flesh-and-blood biographical Rodriguez. Rather, it is the Rodriguez entity we grow in our mind when we watch his films; it is the entity we imagine who has the know-how to add and mix ingredients in such a way that they blend together to make something spectacularly new in the world. And the more of his films one sees, the more one generates a complex and complete sense of the implied director Rodriguez. I don't know much about his daily life and only have a very impressionistic sense of what it is like to be on the set with him, but I imagine an implied director entity that has some of the following attributes:

- Works hard yet has tremendous fun making his films because of a certain comfort in knowing what the film as a whole will look like— he has the unique capacity for cutting the film into its final product in his mind—as well as knowing that he has the skill to pull it off, to transform idea and image into actuality.
- Knows what he wants as an end artifact but listens to his actors and crew to be sure all the ingredients cohere as a whole.

- Is modest about himself, placing at a higher value the needs and time of those he works with. In *El Mariachi*, for instance, he worked with nonprofessional actors and was very aware that their time mattered; he would feed lines on the spot, film, then move to the next shot, feed a line, etc.
- Draws actors to his flame because of his skill and his tremendous sense of the playfulness in filmmaking.
- Knows well his audience for each respective film.
- Follows very much the comic-book sensibility. With the exception of *Sin City* I don't mean necessarily that he makes comic-book films in the strict sense, but rather that he brings to his filmmaking that foundational sense of the limitless possibilities and fun seen especially in the Tex Avery–style cartoons.

Given that this anything-goes comic-book sensibility as especially embodied in the Tex Avery cartoon is so foundational to Rodriguez's worldview, let me expand on this briefly here. As children, when reading comic books or watching a Tex Avery cartoon, we experience a sense of comfort in what can seem to be a rather unstable world of adults. As adults living in increasingly dangerous and precarious times, reading comic books and watching a Tex Avery cartoon may also bring a sense of quietude and appeasement and joy. We see this most especially in our experience of comic books that follow a Tex Avery sensibility — and of course in the immersion in the Tex Avery cartoons themselves. No matter the danger encountered (being crushed to a pulp, even) or tragedy experienced (the death of a family member, even), many comic-book protagonists (especially of the superhero variety) bounce back. This claim to a kind of immortality can be especially gratifying and reassuring to children (and teens) who worry constantly about the loss of parents. And, in the world of comics, not even the sky is the limit in terms of what we can do physically (natural laws) and socially (modes of behavior).

This anything-goes sensibility is especially captured in those Tex Avery–created and –directed animations of the early 1940s through mid-1950s — *Droopy* (1943), *Screwball Squirrel* (1944), and *Billy Boy* (1954) — for instance. The independent, unrestricted, highly perceptive worldview present in Avery's animations where characters defy all sorts of natural and social laws embodies also Rodriguez's creative and sovereign approach to filmmaking.

In form and substance Tex Avery's approach to animation differed greatly from that of Walt Disney. Where Disney used his technical means to create cartoons aimed at fostering close adherence to social and natural laws, Avery made cartoonworlds that pushed at the these social and natural boundaries. While Disney sought conventions that would give the illusion of a nontransgressive,

Droopy (1943). The wolf explodes with surprise at Droopy's ability to outsmart him.

conventional reality, Avery's storyworlds aimed at the extremely unconventional, infusing his works with, as Floriane Place-Verghnes states, "a certain poetic and oneiric (of dreams) quality" (5). So, while Disney sought to give his cartoonworlds the smooth and polished veneer of a conventional realism, Avery made cartoonworlds that delighted in the flaunting of their own unbounded possibilities. In Disney, the bad guys are evil in carefully calculated and limited ways, while the good guys are good according to recognized social rules of behavior, and they remain so for all eternity. In Avery, the bad guys are unrestrained rascals and the good guys are sometimes also dangerously mischievous. In Disney animations the animal characters are almost always ascribed human attributes. In Avery we see most animal characters behaving in ways that are socially and physically impossible for humans. Avery's *Screwball Squirrel* (1944) makes the differences crystal clear when Screwy Squirrel beats up the more Disney-like, coy, and happy-go-lucky Sammy Squirrel. When Sammy Squirrel tries to steal the show, telling the audience this is "about me and all my friends in the forest," Screwy Squirrel takes him behind a tree and beats him silly, reasserting the Avery-styled Screwy as the real star of the cartoon.

Of course, technically Avery followed similar rules in terms of perspective, principles of motion, and the use of geometric shapes to give weight and solidity to his characters. However, he used them in the service of pushing the envelope on the creative possibilities of animation. As John Canemaker remarks, Avery "constantly pulled the rug out from under audiences by reversing their expectations regarding the laws of physics or by turning hoary and hallowed fairytales into Rabelaisian sex-and-violence romps" (14). Avery's animations are all body, but in ways that conceive of the body as infinitely malleable, resistant, and not bound by the laws of nature. They might squeeze through keyholes, explode into fragments to express surprise, but they swiftly reunify into their respective wholes once again.

To sum up: In watching Rodriguez's films we discern an implied director entity that is at once considerate of his crew and actors, all-knowing (able to see the cut film in his mind even before production begins), hard-working, and eminently open to learning new technologies to push at the filmmaking envelope. Last, this implied director entity is oriented toward the absorption and effective use in filmmaking of the playful, adventurous, and absolutely free spirit found in many comic books—and superbly and paradigmatically present in creator and director Tex Avery's animations—that allows the audience to experience a total immersion in the deepest recesses of their sovereign imagination.

ANYTHING GOES, WITHIN REASON

Anything can happen in Rodriguez's films, just as anything can happen in comics, cartoons—and *dreams*. In a dream one might sweat and pant when hunted by a monster, but just before it grabs for a leg or arm, it turns out that one has the power to fly. In *El Mariachi* Rodriguez uses, as the main motor of the plot, the Mariachi double (or doppelgänger)—the kind of experience of a double of ourselves that we have in our dreams. In *Machete* the character Shé (Michelle Rodriguez) takes a bullet in the eye, then reappears with an eye patch ready for battle; a bullet already lodged in Machete's (Danny Trejo) skull stops another bullet from killing him; under the rules that govern our non-comic-book biology, in *Machete Kills* (2013) Machete should not have survived being lynched or shot with a .38—yet again. Rodriguez asks that the viewer enter a storyworld where daydreaming and wishful thinking rule and all disbelief is suspended.

We see this anything-goes, comic-book, Tex Avery–cartoon approach already very early on in Rodriguez's filmmaking. We see this already with the short, ten-minute film "Halloween IV" that he made as a teenager. Here he uses the computer graphics available at the time (1985) to create an animated character that explodes to introduce the production credit (Video Slug) and ready the audience for a story that at once admixes violence (murder by pounding of nails into foreheads, leaping onto strategically placed pitchforks, or pitchfork through arterial veins, for instance) with the comic (exaggerated sound effects and facial expressions, for instance). Shot on a VHS camera and edited on VHS decks along with a careful orchestration of sound score, the young Rodriguez creates a ten-minute short film where anything can happen—and that takes us through a range of positive and negative emotions. He also includes outtakes—a choice that, while prevalent with the spread of DVD technology, was a rather unusual occurrence during this period of film history. I think only of Hal Needham's films like *Hooper* (1978) and the *Smokey and the Bandit* trilogy (1980–1984). We see this same careful attention to casting, orchestration of body language, sound, editing, and lensing in his longer film also made during this period, "Miami Priest." With this one he also includes what would become a trademark: the announcing of a "Coming Soon" film. Of course, with bigger budgets he can create actual trailers of films that he has yet to make (as with *Machete* and *Machete Kills*), but this doesn't stop him from whetting the appetite of his audience here by including the title "Priest Wars IV" as coming soon.

Rodriguez's Tex Avery worldview and technique comes into its own in his 1990 short, "Bedhead." The film unfolds as follows: after awaking from a concussion, the protagonist and voice-over narrator Rebecca (Rebecca Rodriguez, who would later step into the shoes of editor with *Machete* and coeditor with Robert on *Machete Kills* and would be credited as a coproducer on *Spy Kids 4D*) can make her slob and bully of a brother she nicknames "Bedhead" (David Rodriguez) do things clearly against his will, like kiss her feet or hit his head against a pole; she suddenly has the strength and power to lasso his feet and drag him behind her bicycle, pedaling at ninety miles an hour. The film participates, as Charles Ramírez Berg identifies, in the "childhood empowerment narrative" ("Ethnic Ingenuity" 109). However, as Ramírez Berg counters, unlike films such as *Home Alone* (1990), where the child assimilates to the adults' usually conservative worldview, in "Bedhead" Rodriguez offers a "counterhegemonic Chicano variation" (109). In so many words, Ramírez Berg considers how Rebecca's "magic" and "raised consciousness" (she mentions how she could bring peace to the Middle East) stand against an adult world filled with rules and prejudices that straightjacket possibilities of being a young Latina in the world.

I would add that Rodriguez brings his comic-book sensibility to the making of "Bedhead"—one that ends up weaving itself throughout all his films. Just as when Screwy Squirrel beats to a pulp Sammy Squirrel or as happens when Wile E. Coyote is flattened by a boulder, no real physical harm is done. Serious and dangerous things can happen to the characters, but they come through without a scratch. We empathize immediately with Rebecca and her siblings. And, just as Rebecca is upset at her slob of a brother's actions—eating his cereal

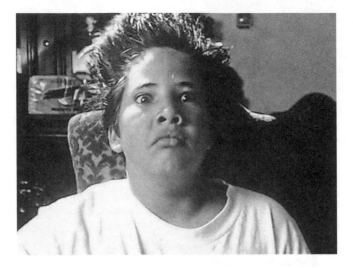

"Bedhead" (1990). The bully brother known as "Bedhead" at breakfast.

like a pig—and so wishes bad things to happen to him, like Rebecca, the audience doesn't really want mean things to happen to him. So Rodriguez invites us to share in Rebecca's wish (or daydream) to have him punished, but in a cartoonish way. Whatever happens will have no significance; whether this is dragging a brother behind a bike at ninety miles an hour or trying to bring to earth his seemingly gravity-defiant hair, nothing ultimately happens to the brother except that he now treats the sister with a certain respect.

We see in all Rodriguez's films the use of a variety of opening sequences to establish respective viewer contracts; in "Bedhead," he uses a preface or prologue-like animation sequence to establish this anything-goes contract. This at once introduces the film's opening credits and establishes this contract with the viewer: silent-era, Chaplinesque, zany, madcap music plays over a caricature of a cockroach running from a boy's hand that grabs, squeezes, then swallows him whole (as happens in the film). The boy burps the title, "Bedhead." Even before the story proper begins, Rodriguez has established the playful mood as well as cartoon-like conventions that the filmgoer will encounter once in the storyworld. The filmgoer who signs on and continues to watch the film will have the pleasure of engaging with characters whose actions defy the logic of physics (Rebecca's telekinesis, for instance) and the social (a sister with greater power over an otherwise bully of a brother).

I should say that while Rodriguez often uses the space before the story proper begins as a prologue of sorts to establish this contract—in *Desperado* and *Once Upon a Time in Mexico*, it is in the form of the bar talk—it is not always the case. For instance, with *El Mariachi* the viewer is thrown right into the middle of the story; the low buzz and wind sounds establish an ominous feel and mood followed by some slow-motion action shots of hit men loading their guns and machine gun fire. This establishes the texture and mood of the *narcotraficante* genre. Only after the opening credits appear seven minutes into the film is the cartoon sensibility established: the comical effect of using fast motion while portraying the female police officer standing, then sitting again when Azul (Reinol Martínez) pays her off. Rodriguez uses this Chaplinesque quick motion technique throughout to remind the viewers of the film's cartoon-like sensibility.

Rodriguez uses the different devices, including casting actors who do well in their facial gestures and body language to convey a comic-book sensibility, to open the space to the limitless possibilities offered by the dream-like worldview of cartoons. Paradoxically, this creating of a cartoon-like sense of "anything goes" is done precisely in Rodriguez's careful exercise of his logic capacity—his causal and counterfactual imagining—in the making of films where the logic of "anything is possible" predominates. There is a coherence and consistency in Rodriguez's approach and worldview: this is the worldview that is presented over and over again in different forms and guises in all his films.

Rodriguez's anything-goes cartoon-like sensibility reminds us of the essential function of fiction film: that we do not go to the cinema to learn history, sociology, politics, and so on. While we recognize emotions and actions of the siblings, we don't learn anything new about actual reality when watching "Bedhead." Neither do we learn anything new about the first few years of the twenty-

"Bedhead" (1990). The opening: the animation sequence when a character burps the word "Bedhead."

first century when we watch any of the *Spy Kids* films. Nor are we moved emotionally, under the influence of any of these *Spy Kids* films, to defend, say, the cause of the exploitation of Fooglies (odd-looking transmogrified humans who speak backward). We recognize the set of emotions experienced by teenagers (insecurities, jealousies, desires) in *Roadracers* (1994), but Rodriguez's use of lensing (close-ups and wide angles, for instance) to capture extreme facial and body gestures of the protagonist Dude Delaney (David Arquette)—and these become even more exaggerated and menacing as the story reaches its denouement—reminds the viewer that this film—any film, actually—is not the same as reality. Rather, Rodriguez chooses to give his characters schematic shape by painting them with huge brush strokes and endowing them with cut-and-dried personality traits. He distills necessarily the complex operations of human beings.

The everyday life functioning of the brain is messy, complicated, and mixed. It is shapeless in every way, except in its functions governed by laws of nature (physics, biology, etc.). When Rodriguez chooses to distill human behavior, he chooses to give fictional *shape* to this otherwise messy behavior. Rodriguez's particular choices in this shape-giving activity, triggered and guided by aesthetic goals in his creating of aesthetic artifacts (film object), are to create certain emotional and cognitive, affective and rational responses or reactions to the products of his work. So, for a film like *Roadracers* to work, all we know *and need to know* about Dude is that he wants to get out of town.

This is what Rodriguez's art is: the distillation and reorganization of the building blocks of reality (emotions included) to make something new that we don't confuse with reality. Indeed, the awe-producing activity of Rodriguez as a filmmaker is precisely that he is able to select those psychological traits most relevant to the development of the story and that will reverberate in the viewer's memory long after the final credits roll. As his films remind in their form, content, and outlook, we go to see Rodriguez's films to experience a carefully orchestrated fictional blueprint that satisfies our need for fiction.

THE BROWNING OF AMERICA

Rodriguez exists within a larger U.S. Latino filmmaking tradition, which includes notables such as Gregory Nava, Edward James Olmos, Luis Valdez, Lourdes Portillo, Ramón Menendez, Jesús Salvador Treviño, Peter Bratt, Cheech Marin, and Alex Rivera, among others. At the same time, he represents a new generation of Latino filmmaker—one that doesn't necessarily only include in its focus explicitly, say, Latino issues: generational divisions and assimilation seen in, for instance, Luis Valdez's *La Bamba* (1987)—and even more so in Gregory Nava's *Mi Familia* (1995); disenfranchisement and sense of non-citizen status (socioeconomic) that leads to a life of gangbanging in Allison Anders's *Mi Vida Loca* (1993) and Edward James Olmos's *American Me* (1992); exploitation and oppression in the urban environs such as in Gregory Nava's *El Norte* (1984) or in the fields as told through the lens of Paul Espinosa's . . . *and the earth did not swallow him* (1995); the satiric social critique Cheech Marin levels at the U.S. mainstream and policy makers in *Born in East LA* (1987); or the more recent look to the U.S./Mexico borderlands and the global patriarchal, capitalist system that allows for the ravaging of young Latinas in Gregory Nava's *Bordertown* (2006) and the cyber-transborder exploitation of Latinos in Rivera's *Sleep Dealer* (2008).

Several film scholars have used broad-brush strokes to characterize these and other films that make up the corpus of Latino cinema. Such a cinematic tradition, Chon Noriega remarks, "seeks to define difference [. . .] against the backdrop of the 'non-Chicano,' and it does so in the name of an ethnic nation, community, or culture" (*Shot in America* xxxi). It is this same impulse to identify films that work *against* the grain of mainstream cinema, and more, that we see with Rosa-Linda Fregoso. She includes Latina filmmakers such as Lourdes Portillo to complicate what this, say, difference looks like; it might not be a difference visible as set against the mainstream, but rather one where the difference (gender, for instance) is made apparent within the portrayal of the Chicano community itself. In this sense, too, for Fregoso, Chicano cinema has grown out of its persistent connection to issues of opposition and exploitation; thus it is a tradition that necessarily requires a sociopolitical purview in its interpretation.

Other scholars aim to give a certain order to the broad-brush strokes. Gary Keller and Charles Ramírez Berg offer a number of classifications. With an eye to the different periods in which Latino documentary and feature film directors have used an "anti-stereotyping aesthetic" (*Latino Images in Film* 5) to resist, overturn, and complicate Hollywood's stereotypical representations, Ramírez Berg establishes categories according to historical periods. For instance, he considers films made between 1969 and 1976 as part of the first wave of Latino filmmaking; this first wave of films is the most overtly political and oppositional; it is most closely tied to the Chicano cultural nationalist movement (*Latino Images in Film* paraphrase 185). Walking on the heels of the first wave, he identifies the making of films with a "rebellious, not separatist" politics (186). While this second wave of films is laced with anger, it is, he remarks, "channeled into more accessible forms" (186) such as Valdez's *Zoot Suit* (1981), Robert Young's *The Ballad of Gregorio Cortez* (1982), Peter Travers's *A Time to Remember* (1987), and Nava's *El Norte* (1988). Overlapping chronologically with the second wave, Ramírez Berg identifies a third wave with the appearance of films in the 1980s and gaining visible momentum in the 1990s (made either within or outside the Hollywood system) that sidesteps emphasis on oppression, exploitation, or resistance. He gives many examples, including Rodriguez's "Bedhead" and *El Mariachi*. It is a period when we see Latino-ness simply as a matter of fact, and not something put under a spotlight. Ethnicity simply *is*. In this third wave of Latino cinema, as Ramírez Berg states, "political content is embedded within the deeper structure of the genre formulas the filmmakers employ rather than being on the surface" (187).

Whether sociopolitical or formalist in approach, the scholars of Latino cinema one way or another focus on issues of representation. It is not surprising that this continues to be the hot-button subject for scholars of Latino film. While Latinos exert a huge demographic weight in the United States at fifty-plus million and counting, our presence in the media is still very slim; and this thin presence continues to follow closely yesteryear's stereotypes: preternaturally hot tempered, violent, and ravenously sexual. Indeed, as Mary Beltrán discovers, while we see sprinkles of Latinas appearing in "interesting and compelling roles" (108), the general trend is that they continue to be held fast to the spitfire stereotype. (See also essays collected in Keller; Noriega, *Chicanos and Film*; Noriega and López.)

It is certainly the case that Rodriguez represents a new model of Latino filmmaking, one whereby the director can (1) choose to completely make natural the presence of a character's Latino ethnicity—it simply *is* as it *is* for Anglo characters in most films; (2) cast Latino actors in Latino roles—or any other role; and (3) choose to highlight Latino identity in ways that playfully foreground or overturn the stereotypes. With regard to casting, Rodriguez insisted on casting the then unknown Salma Hayek in *Roadracers*. Hayek was written into an unproduced screenplay *Till Death Do Us Part* (coauthored with Alvaro Rodriguez), but the project was abandoned, so Rodriguez placed her front and center in *Roadracers*. (Several written sequences from *Till Death Do Us Part* were brought to life in *Spy Kids* and *Once Upon a Time in Mexico*.)

In addition to crossing over an unknown (to U.S. audiences) Spanish-speaking telenovela actress (well-known in Mexico as the lead in *Teresa*), Rodriguez also insisted that the Hollywood-produced action/Western, *Desperado*, include a large Latino cast. Indeed, Latino actors such as Hayek, Danny Trejo, Cheech Marin, and Antonio Banderas, among others, appear again and again in all his films; the filmmaking increasingly under his total control, he would later cast Latina Jessica Alba to play the Irish stripper in *Sin City*. With respect to Rodriguez's choosing to highlight Latino identity in ways that playfully foreground or overturn the stereotypes, Ronald L. Mize and Grace Peña Delgado write of how, in Rodriguez's *Machete*, for instance, he combines and subverts Latina stereotypes in his characterization of "hyper-sexualized, hyper-violent anti-heroines" (167). They comment more generally on his "graphic novel" approach to film and his "over-the-top portrayals of violence and stereotypes" (167) that poke fun at and parody misrepresentations and prejudices circulating in the mainstream. Markus Heide considers how Rodriguez's films Mexicanize or Latino-ize the American road-movie, Western, and horror movie genres. He writes, "Rodriguez's career seems to be characteristic of the observation that 'ethnic cinema' has meanwhile moved to Hollywood, and that the relation between formerly exclusive categories such as 'commercially successful' and 'politically engaged' has become more complex in recent years" (262). In Rodriguez's latest move to shake up the representational map, he is helming Comcast's channel, El Rey Network (his proposal beat out one hundred others submitted to Comcast), which features Latino actors and public figures in its round-the-clock English-language programming, including reality and scripted shows, animation, feature films, documentaries, news, music, and sports programming. As already mentioned, Alvaro Rodriguez, fiction author, cowriter on several of Robert Rodriguez's films, and Rodriguez's cousin, is one of the writers of *From Dusk till Dawn*, the TV series for El Rey Network.

URBAN LATINO

Largely urban-dwelling, English-speaking (and secondarily Spanish) Latinos are driving the population growth in the United States. It is this demographic that is also pushing up buying power dollar numbers into the trillions; today, the U.S. Latino market ranks as the twelfth largest economy in the world. (See Espinoza.) In many ways Rodriguez embodies this demographic shift and growth.

Rodriguez is a third-generation Latino who comes of age as a filmmaker during a particularly huge growth spurt in the U.S. Latino population. Latinos are the largest minority in this country. Latinos are one in every six people — or approximately fifty million, not including the undocumented. After Mexico, the United States has the largest Latino population in the world. This is a young and growing population. It is a largely urban population. It is a huge audience interested in and engaged with all variety of media, including film, television, video games, comic books, and the like. At any given time, there are forty-eight million Latinos watching television, according to the Nielsen ratings; and Latino children and teens outnumber all other ethnic groups when it comes to playing video games.

Rodriguez is part of this Latino demographic—a demographic with *an urban worldview*. For a long time, Latinos lived and worked in the countryside, with little time, energy, and inclination to create in any considerable dimension works of art (literature, plastic and other arts, music, film) and/or engage in them. For instance, art that one could produce without much cost—literature, artisan-crafted art, and the like—was done by a handful of Latinos, and their viewers/audience/readers were scarce. When towns and cities started to grow at an accelerated pace in America toward the end of the nineteenth century and the beginning of the twentieth century, the cultural environment of the country changed. People in the entertainment industry became legion, and the number of authors grew exponentially. After the Second World War the Latino population increased evermore and settled mainly in large towns and cities, where their economic life shifted from agriculture to factory production and consumer industries. This shift brought about new lifestyles and new world-views, with more time for leisure and entertainment and a will to overcome the alienation and anonymity associated with urban life. Urbanization also meant, then, cultural renewal, and the rapid development of the taste for narrative fiction in the format of film.

In many ways, what Ramírez Berg and the other scholars mentioned above describe is the creating of a Latino cinema by filmmakers who could make a living crafting films with a mass audience in mind. That is, we see in the 1980s and 1990s the beginning of filmmakers' living and working in cities also filled with more and more Latinas and Latinos. These urban-dwelling Latinos cultivated a range of behaviors and tastes, as well as values and cognitive development that were now more and more heavily marked by an urban environment, at both the individual and collective levels. Their new reality became infinitely complex. In this new environment, more and more Latinos aspired to become filmmakers (among many other possibilities such as comic-book makers, novelists, poets, and the like). In the 1980s and 1990s, Latino cinema became more and more instrumental as a safe and trusted guide in the affective and intellectual urban maze. And their audience kept growing constantly and ever more diversified, so they could accommodate what are generally called highbrow, middlebrow, and lowbrow cultural products.

Rodriguez doesn't create films in a sociocultural, economic, or historical void. He came of age as a filmmaker the moment certain social and economic conditions were met and Latino artists and their products *emerged* in a continuous and varied way. Rodriguez is the apotheosis of this trend. His films fall into any and all categories (high, low, middle) and touch on any and all subjects: Latino spy kids to Irish strippers to Gatling-gun amputees to vengeful Mexican ex-*federales*.

Rodriguez's life very much reflects the growing of this generation of Latinos with an urban worldview: massively diversified in its cultural products and tastes. Born June 20, 1968, Rodriguez grew up in a large family (nine siblings) in the urban environment of San Antonio, Texas. His father, Cecilio, worked as a traveling salesman; he sold cookware, china, and crystal. His mother, Rebecca, worked as a nurse. The education of Rodriguez's varied film tastes started early. He learned to play the guitar and the saxophone. And, living in an urban environment offered the possibility of the mother's taking the children to the movies at the local *barrio* (or neighborhood) revival house, the Olmos Theatre. In an interview with Peter Travers he recalls how "we'd sit with food hidden under diapers and watch movies two or three times" ("On the Move with Robert Rodriguez" 47). Rodriguez would watch double and sometimes triple features, including the films of the Marx Brothers to those of Hitchcock. In *Rebel Without a Crew*, he considers these outings to be some of the most significant of his early childhood memories.

It seems Rodriguez was not the only sibling to grow a passion for the arts: film and music, especially. His sister Elizabeth Rodriguez became an actress, appearing in *Desperado* as the Mariachi fan. His sister Patricia Vonne grew up to become a professional actress and musician; she's cut several albums and has appeared in *El Segundo* and *Heavenly Beauties*, as well as in several of Rodriguez's films, including *Spy Kids*, *Sin City* (as the character Dallas), and *Desperado* (a bar girl), and he includes her song "Traeme Paz" in *Once Upon a Time in Mexico*. His sister Angela Lanza also became an actress and musician, appearing in *Fools Rush In* and in *The Perez Family*, where she performs "Yo Soy El Punto Cubano"; she makes an appearance in *Spy Kids* and *Spy Kids 2*. And, as I already mentioned, his sister Rebecca had a hand in editing *Machete* and coediting *Machete Kills*.

Rodriguez's early fascination with those films seen at the Olmos Theatre was really an interest in the way photos cut together could create a continuous sense of motion. While the technology was clearly out of reach economically for the young Rodriguez, already in the fifth grade he had begun experimenting with this by giving motion to static, cartoon images that he drew at the edges of a used paperback dictionary that he owned. In *Rebel* he recalls the making of flip cartoon movies with elaborate seemingly invisible characters that would bounce "around and off the pages, battling evil, and blowing up everything in sight" (vii). While Rodriguez would continue to hone his cartooning craft in high school and then college, it was a desire to make motion out of photographs, or create stories out of motion photography, that continued to grow.

He first tried his hand at making a stop-motion live action film with his father's Super 8 camera, but this proved too technologically unfriendly. Then his father came home with a new four-head JVC videocassette recorder and camera. He had bought the equipment with the idea of making a sales presentation. However, Rodriguez got his hands on the equipment and began shooting videos of everything, including clay animations and short action comedies with his siblings. It had an audio dub feature that allowed him to erase then rerecord sound over the films; he learned to edit with the camera and how to lay the music over later. To make the visual and audio synching easier, he also learned to shoot as little footage with as few takes as possible. To become more and more efficient at this, he trained himself more and more to see, as he states, "the movie edited in my head beforehand" (*Rebel* x).

In 1981, the same year that George Miller's *The Road Warrior* (the second film in the *Mad Max* series) was released, so too was John Carpenter's *Escape from New York*—a film that Rodriguez, his cousin Alvaro, and several of their friends managed to see. As Alvaro Rodriguez so gracefully puts it in the Afterword to my edited volume, *Critical Approaches to the Films of Robert Rodriguez*, they escaped the "sweltering South Texas heat" not only to immerse themselves in the storyworld of Manhattan-Island-cum-maximum-security-prison but for Rodriguez to catalogue for Alvaro's "eager ears a run-through of how Carpenter shot this sequence and that, already informing what would become his own style" (forthcoming). That Carpenter wrote, shot, and scored the film solidified in Rodriguez the ambition to become a filmmaker. Moreover, with the growing presence of video stores during this period, Rodriguez's access to movies allowed for this autodidactic impulse to flourish. The traditional ways of seeing and studying films at the cinema or in film schools could be sidestepped. Video stores allowed easier access to movies, and the VHS equipment with its pause, rewind, and fast-forward functions allowed Rodriguez to study closely directors that caught his eye. This early home schooling in film would later come to shape his uses and reshaping of techniques and conventions from all over the directorial map.

He continued to hone his filmmaking (and cartooning) craft while attending St. Anthony's High School Seminary, a private high school in San Antonio. It was here that Rodriguez would meet another aspiring filmmaker, Carlos Gallardo. Both wanted to become better and better filmmakers. Years before they would go on to make *El Mariachi*, Rodriguez and Gallardo traveled to Acuña, Mexico, to make the Indiana Jones–inspired *Ismael Jones and the Eyes of the Devil* (circa 1984)—but this time around with a Latino (Gallardo) saving the day and getting the gal. Both gravitated toward the action feature film. Gallardo made the short action film *The Guy from the Land Down Under*, and Rodriguez continued to sharpen his skills making shorts and trailers and working (unpaid) as the designated film guy for the high school football games; even in the latter he became quickly known for his creativity—shooting audience expressions and focusing on spiraling footballs instead of the action on the field. Beginning in his sophomore year and ending in his senior, Rodriguez made several short films—they took the place of having to write final term papers. They include a couple of the films mentioned earlier such as the ten-minute "Priest Wars" (the end of his sophomore year, 1984), the fifteen-minute "Beverly Hills Priest" (the end of his junior year film, 1985), and the twenty-seven-minute "Miami Priest" (the end of his senior year, 1986).

The University of Texas at Austin, where Rodriguez enrolled in 1986, would prove to be more than just a place for higher-minded learning and thinking. It became yet another training ground for Rodriguez as a comic strip author/artist (his popular "Los Hooligans" strip based on his siblings ran in the *Daily Texan* for three consecutive years) and as a filmmaker. UT Austin housed the very well regarded and extremely competitive Department of Radio-Television-Film (RTF). Rodriguez knew that to take his craft to the next level, he had to be able to train on 16mm cameras. Working three jobs while carrying a full load, however, didn't serve his GPA well. With only thirty spots open and one hundred applicants, he knew he would have to use other means to open the door to the RTF program. On his own time and using borrowed Super 8 and video recording camera equipment and then a camcorder that he bought with money he earned from a cholesterol experiment and then antidepressant drug studies, he made a series of shorts he anthologized under the title *Austin Stories*. He sent them out to small film festivals. They picked up several awards, including those of the Austin CableVision video contest as well the Eighth Annual Third Coast Film and Video Competition sponsored by the Texas Union at the University of Texas at Austin. *The Austin Chronicle*'s founder and editor, Louis Black, happened to be one of the judges; after witnessing his extraordinary filmmaking skills, Black quickly became one of Rodriguez's earliest supporters.

Not only did *Austin Stories* pick up numerous accolades (and some airtime on PBS), but it ended up opening the door to the much coveted RTF program at UT Austin. He showed the films to Steve Mims, who taught production in the RTF department. His homegrown low-tech video making and editing skills—and self-discipline and perseverance—paid off. He was admitted into the RTF program—by other means. In the RTF program Rodriguez grew the support and admiration of Mims and also the seminal Latino film theorist Charles Ramírez Berg. Enrollment in the program also gave Rodriguez the access to the 16mm camera equipment he longed to put through its paces; he wanted to push the technology to its limit to see everything it could do in the making of what would become his short film "Bedhead."

It was during this period that Rodriguez met Venezuela-born, Houstonraised Elizabeth Avellán. One of Rodriguez's jobs on campus was as a file clerk in the provost's office where Avellán was working as an administrative associate for executive vice president and provost Gerhard Fonken. They married, and she would use her administrative and budget management skills to act as producer of his films. Later, while Rodriguez was working in LA on *Roadracers*, Avellán met Hollywood producer Debra Hill, who became a "mentor to Avellán" and helped her find her way into graduate-level production courses at UCLA's extension program (Macor 143).

With the success of his $800-made short "Bedhead" Rodriguez figured out that even if he used a 16mm camera with its more expensive film stock, if he used the same shooting and editing techniques that he used with "Bedhead" he could make a feature film for $7,000. (By this time, he had already made nearly thirty short narrative films.) Checking himself in for more drug clinical trials (with ruled index cards, notepad, and a copy of Stephen King's *Dead Zone*), Rodriguez earned part of the money (Gallardo also contributed) to make the film. As Ramírez Berg already mentioned in the Foreword, with a borrowed Arriflex 16mm Rodriguez and Gallardo went south of the border to make the film. The idea was to make a film to sell to the Spanish-language video market—to make an inexpensive feature length film that he could, as he remarks, "quietly fail on, and learn from my mistakes" (*Rebel* 4). With only fourteen days of borrowed time on the Arriflex, they went straight to Ciudad Acuña, where Gallardo had family connections and where they might piggyback off of resources available via Alfonso Arau's crew, who were filming *Like Water for Chocolate*; Rodriguez also borrowed props from Arau's set like the bathtub featured in *El Mariachi*.

At a fever pitch, Rodriguez shot *El Mariachi* in just shy of fourteen days (as it turned out, the Arriflex was needed back on Day 13) and for the budgeted $7,000. After much hard work editing and synching the sound, he was ready to peddle his wares in LA. Rodriguez recounts this part of the story much better than I could in *Rebel Without a Crew*, but suffice it to say that pounding pavement along with some good fortune led to his signing on with Robert Newman from the ICM talent agency. Rodriguez didn't sell *El Mariachi* to the Spanish video market. Rather, by April 1992 Newman had used it to lasso a film deal with Columbia: the $7 million budgeted follow-up, *Desperado*, along with national distribution of *El Mariachi*. (See Macor.) In *Rebel* he remarks, "The main reason was that I wanted to make a modestly budgeted Hollywood picture with a Latino action hero, something I'd always wanted to see in movies since I was a kid" (194). After a $100,000 investment in a 35mm blowup of *El Mariachi*, it went on to gross $5 million—and an additional $1.5 million with its English dubbed VHS version that sold in the video market. *El Mariachi* was also credited as boosting the indie-film scene of the 1990s. It was during this flurry of activity that Rodriguez would also meet another coconspirator on filmmaking projects—Quentin Tarantino.

Importantly, Rodriguez's early experiences with making *Desperado* identified potential hazards in his road. Hollywood didn't like that he wrote, directed, edited, and even operated the Steadicam in making *Desperado*. He remarks, for instance, how "it was a battle with the studio for them to let me edit my own movie. The reason? They just weren't used to having a director edit his own picture" (194). He took note and did what was necessary for him to be owner of his talents, time, and whereabouts. It was crystal clear: He wanted his filmmaking to be based out of Austin, and he wanted as much control over the filmmaking as possible.

After wrapping *Desperado* (1995) Rodriguez did what others thought impossible. He moved in quick succession to make "The Misbehavers" segment of *Four Rooms* (released in 1995) and then to direct the Tarantino-scripted road/comic-book gore flick, *From Dusk till Dawn* (released in 1996). "I knew people would be watching for that sophomore slump, so I figured that instead of making one film and putting all the eggs in one basket, I would simply confuse the marketplace by putting out four films quickly" (*Rebel* 195). His career would prove him to be a director of independent mind who would challenge himself again and again, learning HD, then 3-D, CGI, previsualization animatics, green screen, and monochromatic techniques, for instance. Time and again he proved that he was a director who could create cost-effective, innovative films (reboots, franchises, and mash-ups) that would sell—and well.

Already by 1996, Rodriguez had *El Mariachi* and *Desperado* and *From Dusk till Dawn* under his belt. *Hispanic* had launched him to the top of the list of the "25 Most Powerful Hispanics in Hollywood," squeezing out Banderas, who was second place, and Olmos in third (Avila 20). They identified him as the most promising Latino—the one to look for in the future. In 2010 he received the Austin Film Festival Extraordinary Contribution to Filmmaking Award—with previous honorees including Ron Howard, Danny Boyle, and Oliver Stone. In 2011 *El Mariachi* was added to the Library of Congress's National Film Registry.

In 1995, just after wrapping *From Dusk*, the first member of Rodriguez's family would arrive: Rocket Valentino Rodriguez Avellán. Contracts that were signed allowed him to have greater control over the making of his films and his time for family. Racer Maximiliano Rodriguez Avellán was born in 1997. Rebel Antonio Rodriguez arrived in 1999, Rogue Joaquin Rodriguez in 2004, and Rhiannon Elizabeth Rodriguez in 2005. While in the past he would do much of his editing in "Los Cryptos" (The Crypts) that adjoins his twelve-room, castle-like house (he dreamed this up as a kid) complete with turrets and secret passageways perched high above the Pedernales River on his sixty-three-acre ranch, today, most of the preproduction, production, and postproduction of his films takes place at Troublemaker Studios; the studios are converted airport hangars that lie at the eastern edge of Austin.

Rodriguez would continue to make adult-fare sci-fi/horror mash-ups, but with family so near as his inspiration, he would also go on to make his hugely successful *Spy Kids* films and the Racer-inspired (eight at the time) *Sharkboy and Lavagirl* and Rebel-inspired *Shorts*. (For more on this, see Tauber and Cosgriff.) Today, Rodriguez—along with Richard Linklater and Mike Judge (the animation and feature film director Rodriguez casts as Donnagon Giggles in the first three *Spy Kids* films)—has helped transform Austin into a hub of activity for filmmaking. His Troublemaker Studios (formerly Los Hooligans Productions) is a small industry of cultural production. Rodriguez produced films such as Nimród Antal's sci-fi *Predators* (2010), made mostly at Troublemaker Studios. He produced and created advertising spots such as Nike's "The Black Mamba" (a six-minute mini-film, actually) with Kobe Bryant, who, as Black Mamba, vanquishes his foes: Danny Trejo and Kanye West. Troublemaker Publishing publishes books attached to the films, such as Rodriguez's coauthored book with Racer, *Sharkboy and Lavagirl: The Movie Storybook*, as well as books on the making of *Sin City* and the *Grindhouse* double-bill.

As I will show in the following sections, Rodriguez holds true to his mariachi filmmaking mantra: to maintain creative freedom, to use as few dollars as possible to make the best damned film possible. In *Rebel* he states:

> What is a movie anyway? It's simply a creative endeavor. The more creativity you can apply to solving your problems the better the movie can be. Problems come up all the time no matter how big a budget you have. But on a big-budget movie, a problem arises and since a movie studio's pockets are deep, money is readily available. So, the problem isn't usually solved creatively, instead the problem is washed away quickly with the money hose. (198)

Rodriguez knows well how to use the craft of filmmaking to create low-cost new stories that appeal to his many different, yet very specified and targeted, audiences.

Good, Bad, Ugly ... and Beautiful

*I*N THE SUMMER AND FALL OF 1991 RODRIGUEZ SHOT (IN Acuña, Mexico) then edited (in Austin, Texas) his first feature-length film, *El Mariachi*. While its run time of eighty minutes was considerably longer than his film-fest circuit hit, "Bedhead," his approach was similar: to shoot a feature-length film as inexpensively as possible, but to convey a higher–production value feel and look. To do so meant shooting in as short a period as possible with borrowed camera equipment and inexpensive sound recording devices, using local nonprofessional actors (in this case, townspeople and not siblings), and editing rough (home VHS equipment) and final cuts (free time at an Austin TV studio). The aim: to learn to shoot a feature-length film for little money.

Rodriguez intended to learn how to make a feature-length film by shooting the film. He intended to recoup the $7,000 he would spend making it by selling it to a Spanish-language home-video audience. So, it would take shape in the format of a Mexican narco-drama, or *narcotraficante* film. And, if all worked according to the plan, he would make several more low-budget films that would fund a feature-length film to be used to break into higher-production film-making. For unknowns, the common strategy at the time would be to have an indie film picked up at Sundance by the big studios. Recall, the early 1990s Sundance was the portal for young independent directors to make it big. (In 1991, the Sundance-winning *Sex, Lies, and Videotape* put Steven Soderbergh on the Hollywood map just as *Reservoir Dogs* had for Quentin Tarantino.) Rodriguez's plan did not quite work out as he had anticipated. As I sketched above, it turned out even better.

With Carlos Gallardo and several of Acuña's locals as actors and crew, he shot twenty-five rolls of film (or 25,000 feet) on a borrowed Arriflex 16mm camera with its Kinoptic wide-angle lens; Keith Kristelis, a friend in the Department of Radio-Television-Film at UT Austin, loaned the camera. As it turned out, Kristelis needed the camera back within thirteen days. With such a tight shooting schedule, and on such a slim budget, no film could go to waste and it would all have to be shot in a series of one takes. With the film already cut in his head, he knew what he needed to capture in order to make it into a coherent feature film in the editing room; he knew, for instance, that if he zoomed in on a hand or face, then out again to a middle or long shot, in the editing room, these could be cut together in such a way that it would convey the sense of his using multiple cameras. Indeed, his long practice with shooting and then editing films throughout his teens made this second nature.

The shoot was followed by four months of postproduction work that included editing a rough cut with his own VCR and ProEdit video camera equipment and hours spent synching the sound to the ¾-in. video tapes, and then making the final cut by borrowing Austin's cable access TV facility (ACTV) to edit the film free of charge. In the editing room, he transformed his rough film stock into a kinetic, high-production-feeling feature film with 2,000 cuts.

Rodriguez carefully chose where to make his cuts. The cuts would create the kinetic rhythm that would propel the story forward. They would give the audience a sense that the story is being shown through multiple angles and with different distances to the action; costly Hollywood films often have many cameras filming on the set with the different shots chosen in postproduction. Perhaps most importantly, the cuts would allow him to cover over continuity inconsistencies in the film as well as unconvincing nonprofessional acting. As Sue J. Kim remarks,

> Rodriguez was able to make a film on a shoestring budget by drawing on the fact that our brains have been conditioned to chunk a series of film shots into a coherent narrative whole, with consistent characters (or different ones, in the case of the ranch hand playing multiple bad guys) and plot developments, despite the fact that the filmmakers could not afford proper actors, special effects, equipment, or even a dolly. (198–199)

Given the fast schedule for filming and the availability of equipment, the sound (or auditory channel) making in the film could have presented yet another insurmountable obstacle. However, Rodriguez found a solution. After shooting a scene, he would repeat the scene but without a camera and only his Marantz recorder and Radio Shack mic recording sounds and dialogue that he would synch up in postproduction; as synching proves difficult with dialogue (the sound and the lips moving), this was an additional factor that played into his keeping the dialogue to a minimum. He overcame the problem of synching sound with image — matched by hand — by cutting, as Geoff King notes, "at the point where sound and image began to part company, thus cutting into dialogue scenes sooner than might usually be the case" (160). The lack of resources to light larger spaces led Rodriguez to shoot mostly close and medium shots for indoor sequences; for the few interior shots where he needed artificial lighting, he used two 200-watt work lamps. He used these to create the shadows and edges, especially in the darker interior of the bar.

The film's opening sequence shows the result: within the first thirty seconds of the film, Rodriguez includes five different shots with all variety of angles, making it feel as if he had ten different cameras on the set; he includes a variety of sounds (wind, tires rolling across dirt, car engine, clanking of jail bars, footsteps) to establish the film's suspenseful mood. Or, as Jason Wood sums up of the total effect: "Rodriguez whips the whole shebang along at an enjoyably breakneck and breathless pace, employing an at times dizzying array of zooms, wide-angle lenses, intricately edited set-piece shoot-outs and an inventive understanding of the possibilities of sound design" (78).

Shot, chopped, and scored, El Mariachi was ready to shop. Rodriguez either struck out or wasn't entirely satisfied with the contracts offered by a slew of LA-based companies, including Film-Mex, Cine-Mex, and Mex-American. During this period of knocking on doors, Robert Newman's name was mentioned; he was an agent for ICM (International Creative Management). He dropped off El Mariachi along with "Bedhead." After a chance encounter with Newman where Rodriguez was able to pitch the film and several follow up phone calls, including the request to subtitle the film, by early February 1993 "ICM made Rodriguez an official offer" (Chainsaw 129).

With Newman's representation, Rodriguez quickly became a hot commodity. Columbia Pictures and Miramax came knocking; the former offered to re-edit and blow up the 16mm El Mariachi into a 35mm mainstream exhibitable film, and the latter wanted distribution rights. While its 2,000 cuts made the re-editing process more complex, with Rodriguez overseeing the process, Columbia's post postproduction editing investment of $107,000, a positive test screening response from (Latino) audiences, and a million spent on marketing, it received the green light for a six-city, ninety-screen release for February 26, 1993. (For more on the money spent on the film to get it exhibition-ready, see Pierson.) It was a huge commercial success. As Alison Macor writes, "by the time the movie had wrapped up its North American run, it had grossed more than $2 million. In the summer of 1993 Rodriguez traveled overseas to promote El Mariachi's international release in more than ten countries. Toward the end of the year the film was released on videotape, in both subtitled and dubbed versions, and earned more than $1.5 million in sales" (140).

This was not without risk. After all, the story takes mainstream U.S. audiences south of the border where only Spanish is spoken. It's a film cast with all nonprofessional Latinos. It's a film that was made with an ideal audience in mind who gravitate to the *narcotraficante*, B-film story lines made very cheaply by companies who wanted to make entertaining films outside of the Mexican government's control; in 1983, this controlling appendage would appear as the state-funded Instituto Mexicano de Cinematografía (or IMCINE). Charles Ramírez Berg discusses how often the low-budget films (sometimes filmed two simultaneously and in quick shoots of three to four weeks) would be shot with family members, on ranches owned by family members, using whatever was on hand at the time of shooting as props. (See "Ethnic Ingenuity" paraphrase 113.) Much like the exploitation films of American Independent Productions, these Mexican-made, B-grade films were made quickly with the aim of catching viewer interest and creating films that would manipulate without nuance or subtlety audiences' thoughts and feelings. With the advent of VHS technology, low-budget narco-dramas, along with sci-fi, horror, and luchador (wrestler) films, among others, became much more easily accessible. (In his later films, Rodriguez returns to another stream of the Mexploitation format: those low-budget monster and luchador films of the 1960s and 1970s where directors would use overt discontinuity, protracted exposition, recycled footage, brazen anachronisms, and the requisite insertion of wrestling matches into any point in the narrative.)

Rodriguez's *El Mariachi* sits somewhat uneasily in this tradition of Mexican (and U.S.) exploitation filmmaking writ large. Of course, the film could appeal to this audience—and to one satisfied by a higher production feel, the one that Columbia Pictures was banking its money on. While its intended audience was the *narcotraficante*-themed, Mexican home-video market, Rodriguez's high-production filmmaking skills made it appealing to a larger audience. Its box-office success is testament to this, along with its scholarly critical interpretation and reception.

Many mainstream reviews were caught up in the awe of Rodriguez. One way or another, they wondered how a film made with such little money and with such a modest filmmaker pedigree could be so successful. "Few Bucks, Very Big Bang" runs Richard Corliss's headline in *Time* magazine; after mentioning Rodriguez's generating of funds by becoming a lab rat, Corliss remarks on the technical skill required to create the feel of a "controlled hysteria." In *Rolling Stone*, Peter Travers picks up on the entertainment value of the film, writing how it "won't change your life, but in its own modest way the film earns its place at Sundance by celebrating the joy of making movies at a time when the pressures of the marketplace have damn near squeezed out all the fun" (49). (See also Pinsker.)

Film scholars were more apt to identify the different generic elements that made up the film. Jason Wood, for instance, identifies its genre-crossings as sourced from "the Leone Western, the stunt-fixated Hollywood action flick, Hong Kong martial arts pictures, and the melodramatic and romantic conventions of silent cinema" (78). In Rodriguez's hands, this cross-fertilization results in, Wood continues, "exuberant visual style to parodic but undeniably thrilling and polished effect" (78). Mark Irwin identifies *El Mariachi* as a "post-pop hybrid" film that draws its "power and freshness from the unexpected juxtaposition of the two poles of film style, formalism (which is concerned with artifice) and realism (which strives for objectivity)" (70). Geoff King applauds Rodriguez for not falling into the trap of many aspiring filmmakers who seek to create something with the "slick formal qualities associated with the mainstream" (161). Many such films made on a limited budget "fall short and look like what it is: a cheap imitation" (161). Rather, he celebrates Rodriguez's choice to make a film that is "distinctive and a little bit different" (161).

Ramírez Berg considers its generic structures and themes. He analyzes how the film works as "a *mezcla* of two exploitation genres, the Mexican *narcotraficante* film and the transnational action genre I call the warrior adventure film" ("Ethnic Ingenuity" 111). Ramírez Berg identifies the latter genre as typified by Hong Kong martial arts and Japanese samurai films. *El Mariachi* includes the core elements of the warrior adventure film mode:

1. It centers on "a *lone male protagonist* who possesses *special physical skills.*"
2. There is an adherence to a "*personal code of justice and morality, which he directs toward altruistic ends.*"
3. The protagonist "*undergoes a severe test, involving loss.*"
4. Revenge plays a central role in the motivation of the protagonist; it "*motivates his physical rehabilitation,* wherein he regains the special abilities he once commanded."
5. It includes spiritual rehabilitation that involves the coming into a sense of "the sacredness of all life."
6. The protagonist "*confronts and defeats the ruthless villain (usually a drug lord) in a violent and spectacular duel to the death.*"
    ("Ethnic Ingenuity"; italics his; paraphrase 114–115)

El Mariachi complements these generic thematic elements with its use of technical and intensified sound, exaggerated body movement and facial expression and snaps, and kinetic editing. At the same time, Ramírez Berg suggests, Rodri-

guez's *mezcla* film subverts the warrior adventure storytelling format. Rodriguez casts a Spanish-speaking, culturally rooted Mexican as an action hero with
no physical fighting prowess, asking audiences to reconceive the action hero as
a balladeer. For Ramírez Berg, with *El Mariachi* as the source of creativity and
the embodiment of Mexico and with Mexico long-identified in Hollywood as
the source of corruption, Rodriguez reverses this with writing his drug-lord villain, Moco (booger in Spanish), as an Anglo American.

INDUSTRY

Rodriguez filmed *El Mariachi* in the border town of Acuña, Mexico.
As already mentioned, Acuña was chosen because of Carlos Gallardo's family
connections (his hometown) and also because the town was somewhat used to
film crews with Arau's *Like Water for Chocolate* having wrapped there. Indeed,
before shooting *El Mariachi*, while Gallardo worked for Arau on *Like Water
for Chocolate*, Rodriguez spent his time "videotaping the production and becoming friendly with Arau and his wife [the author, Laura Esquivel]. The couple
watched 'Bedhead,' and Esquivel told Rodriguez that after seeing the short her
husband exclaimed, 'Now this is a muchacho who can direct'" (Macor 118). It
was during this trip that he got the idea to make a film for the Spanish video
market. It was also during this time that he would learn from professional visual
effects artist Raul Falomir, who was working on *Like Water*, how and where to
buy squibs and how to use them to create the special effect sequences where
bodies are riddled with bullets and blood spurts; for the blood, Rodriguez filled
condoms with red dye. The decision to film in Mexico was also driven by economic concerns. Rodriguez could make his film in Acuña without too much
red tape and inexpensively. Careful not to ask too much of those who were vol-
unteering their time, he would often script on the spot, feeding a line or two to
the person playing a character, shoot, and then move to the next line and shot.

Let's keep in mind that Rodriguez does not belong to that tradition of big-
time, deep-pocketed directors from the United States traveling into Mexico as
a kind of economic outsourcing or Anglo fantasy wish-fulfillment experience.
Mexico's cheap, exploitable labor pool has attracted quite a few U.S. directors.
When making *Titanic* (1997), James Cameron went to Baja, California, for Mexican laborers who would build a full-scale replica of the eponymous ship. For
Fat Man and Little Boy (1989), Roland Joffé had a replica of Los Alamos built in
Durango, Mexico. Mexico's jungles and lax environmental policies helped John
McTiernan cut production costs to a minimum in the filming of *Predator* (1987)
and *Medicine Man* (1992). David Lynch cut costs by using Mexico's studios and
landscapes to bring to silver-screen life his 1984 adaptation of *Dune*. Similarly,

Paul Verhoeven found Mexico's landscapes to be appropriately otherworldly for depicting life on Mars in his science-fiction thriller *Total Recall* (1990).

Just as U.S. directors have crossed the border for Mexico's cheaper labor, so too has the border motivated action as an element in plots. Usually, this comes in the shape of an Anglo protagonist crossing the border for some kind of thrill or soul-searching quest. We see this in the form of a morality tale in David Ayer's *Harsh Times* (2005). Ayer's tale is one of redemption for a down-and-out former soldier, Jim Luther Davis (Christian Bale), who suffers from post-traumatic stress disorder caused by a recent special ops mission in the Middle East. He finds his peace in Mexico, a bucolic landscape that provides him the comforts of home cooking and the affectionate arms of his love interest, Marta (Tammy Trull). Marta enchants Jim with her sage-sounding folkloric riddles. And, in *Apocalypto* (2006), Mel Gibson portrays pre-Columbian Mayan life as one of either peace and harmony or chaos and bloodshed. In one, the white man crosses into the arms of bucolic Mexico for spiritual enlightenment, and in the other the white man (Spanish conquistador) arrives to save the primitive Other (the Maya) from destroying one another.

Rodriguez was not making a film from this traditional Hollywood perspective, nor was he in Mexico building the *Titanic*. He was making a low-budget film starring Latinos and whose action hero was a Latino. He was making a film that he hoped would be a stepping-stone to the making of more films with Latinos in any and all variety of roles. Getting attention at Sundance was the usual route; in its inception *El Mariachi* was not going to be that film. That its road would lead to Sundance—and its winning of the Audience Award at the Sundance Film Festival in 1993—was serendipitous. It was also a game changer. It brings Mexican genre film together with high-production action with a mainstream appeal—and, with its Spanish speaking characters necessitating the use of English subtitles, a foreign art-house expectation.

Rodriguez's story of the making of the film nearly eclipsed the film's merits itself. Notably, after ICM signed Rodriguez and studios began to take notice, a Disney producer wanted him to reshoot *El Mariachi* in English and with less ethnic content, specifically changing the protagonist from a Mexican mariachi to an Anglo rock star. (See Ramírez Berg "Ethnic Ingenuity"; Travers.) He went with Columbia (who had signed John Singleton and let him have creative freedom in making *Boyz N the Hood*) to make what would become *Desperado*. Columbia meanwhile insisted on blowing it up for 35mm projection and mainstream consumption. It quickly entered the film history books as the lowest-budgeted movie ever released by a major studio—not to mention that it starred all Latinos and was in Spanish.

With all parts of the filmmaking business in mind, in 1995 Rodriguez went on to publish, with Dutton, *Rebel Without a Crew, or, How a 24-Year-Old Filmmaker* *with $7,000 Became a Hollywood Player.* This not only details the choices he made such as camera placement, lighting, composition, and editing, but how he cut all this together in postproduction to make his film so fresh, dynamic, and cheap. In the same spirit as this book, he often includes, in the DVD-released version of his movies, his "Ten Minute Film School" tips. That is, he wants to share with the world his big secret: creativity and not the proverbial money hose (a term he likes to use) solves problems and usually ends up making better films.

MATTERS OF ENSTRANGEMENT

The opening of *El Mariachi* establishes certain viewing contracts with the audience. Rodriguez intercuts the opening sequence with Azul (Reinol Martínez) breaking out of jail with a parallel sequence of a woman diving into a pool in slow motion and the introduction of the drug lord, Moco, who is on the phone to Azul. In *Border Bandits* Fojas notes the direct allusion to the U.S. drug kingpin Cash Bailey (Powers Boothe) in the Reagan-era-war-on-drugs-released *Extreme Prejudice* (1987)—both gringos living south of the border and whose deaths in both films "puts the business back into the hands of the Mexicans" (120).

The story unfolds, bullets fly, and the audience is introduced to the out-of-towner and out-of-work-wanderer, El Mariachi (Carlos Gallardo). He is confused by the townspeople to be the mid-level narco (drug dealer), Azul (Reinol Martínez). While one is muscled and robust and the other skinny and agile, they both wear black. While contents differ markedly (instruments to kill or to entertain), they both carry guitar cases. This is enough for the resultant identity confusion on the part of the townies and henchmen on the payroll of gringo mob boss, Moco (Peter Marquardt, whom he wrote into the film after meeting him during one of his stints as a proverbial lab rat for a clinical drug trial).

We could go one way with this, asking serious, existential questions such as these: What does it mean to be mistaken for someone else? What does it mean when one's actions are no longer perceived to be one's own, but that of one's doppelgänger—or double? It could be philosophical meditation *and* narco-drama. And, before we see El Mariachi, we hear Gallardo's voice-over: "That morning was just like any other." He then appears visibly on the screen. He continues to muse, "No love. No luck. No ride. Nothing changes. I came across a turtle on the highway. We were both taking our time getting to where we were going. What I didn't know, was that my time . . . was running out." Are we meant to read the turtle symbolically? When he can't find work as a singer and reflects, "My voice is my life," is El Mariachi reflecting on whether our progress (machines like the synthesizer) has also ensured our self-erasure?

El Mariachi (1992). Azul (Reinol Martínez) strutting down a street in
Acuña, Mexico.

Rodriguez does play with the readily identifiable feature of the double, or
doppelgänger. Hector A. Torres considers the doppelgänger function in the
film, but as a doubling of the film *El Mariachi* with the film *Desperado*; the plot
of mistaken identity in the first becomes a plot of revenge in *Desperado*. Torres
writes, "Behind the business of drugs is a dis-formation of the mariachi's original goal, to play guitar and sing like his *antepasados*, his ancestors who were
balladeers in their own times" (166). However, we need not reach out to another film to see how the double functions in *El Mariachi*. The doppelgänger
here works with El Mariachi having, as his other, Azul. But rather than stand as
opposite, they complement one another both in shape (skinny and large) and in
activity (creativity and destruction). Azul and El Mariachi exist in binary unity
as a synthetic double as double protagonists in the film and in antithetical relation to the evil gringo drug lord, Moco—the absolute antagonist. The protagonist–antagonist in their double presence have as their "middle-man" Domino
(Consuelo Gómez). She's the intermediary, the Domino that links Moco with
El Mariachi and Azul as this double as unit.

Rodriguez also intersperses dream sequences into the action. Dream sequences in film conventionally ask audiences to *read* more deeply into the content. When El Mariachi wakes within his dream, he does so on a dirt street
where he sees and hears a little boy (Oscar Fabila) bouncing a basketball. The
thud, thud, thud of the ball hitting the ground is amplified as he bounces the
ball through the deserted town; when he rolls the ball to El Mariachi, it turns
out to be a decapitated head. Rodriguez continues to thread the dream, portraying the boy in a cemetery, a decayed house with only a window frame. In

another sequence, El Mariachi runs through the cemetery with his guitar following Domino, who turns with blood on her face. These slow-motion montage sequences give our brains much to gap fill—or figure out and imagine. They offer a puzzle to solve—something that satisfies the brain. This seems to weigh heavy with symbolic or allegorical significance. Given Rodriguez's film sensibility, it is more likely that these sequences exist to give the emotion system pause to the rapid succession of action sequences—and because of opportunity: the fact of the existence of an interesting looking burned out and decayed house, for instance, and the serendipitous moment of shooting El Mariachi on the side of the road and the turtle's crossing.

More Ed Wood than David Lynch in this sense, the insertion of dreams into his films (recall Wood's opportunistic insertion of surreal, dream-like vignettes in his four-day-shot, 1953 film *Glen or Glenda*) may portend a heavy symbolic or allegorical weight, but this is not the general ambition of the film. Within all this metaphysical, masculine bravado, Rodriguez mixes in the comical; he brings to bear his comic-book trademark sensibility. This is true even within the requisite romancing moment: El Mariachi getting a rubdown in the bath avoids having his private parts (*cojones*) knifed by singing to Domino and her doe-eyed, seemingly nonplussed pit bull. The camera rests for just long enough for the audience to experience a certain incongruity: we expect the pit bull to be aggressive, but it turns out to be more docile than a kitten. Rodriguez's pit bull is nonchalant in the way we expect Tex Avery's dog Droopy to be.

Clearly, Rodriguez wants his audience to understand without fail that this is an exploitation *narco*-drama laced with the warrior adventure story—the film opens with an ominous, synthesized sound and a whistling wind. Yet, he is also careful to remind us that this is very much a story told from a comic-book worldview. Notably, in the opening sequence he introduces pretty quickly the comic-book sensibility: Rodriguez undercranks the camera to make the female police officer's movement and facial expression look jilty and sped up. As Ramírez Berg points out, he uses the camera technique of speeding up action to achieve a "comic effect [. . .] somewhere between Mack Sennett's herky-jerky slapstick and Sam Peckinpah's elegiac lyricism" ("Ethnic Ingenuity" 125). This, of course, is another trick and smart move for Rodriguez to get around working with nonprofessional actors; it's easier for nonprofessional actors to act with broad-brush, caricature-like strokes.

This comic sensibility is expressed with all sorts of techniques and choices. When we see cars moving, we hear exaggerated tires screeching. When we see running around corners, slow motion and close-ups take us right to that moment when boots skid thunderously. When we follow the bartender's finger as he points at a one-man mariachi band with his synthesizer, Rodriguez speeds up the movement to comical effect. To run home the point, Rodriguez creates names that are playfully iconic: Azul (Blue), El Mariachi (the Guitar Player), Moco (or Booger or Snot), and Domino. She is at once the middle tile that joins the others in this game of dominoes, and she has the power to take down all its players, including especially those not on El Mariachi's side.

In so many words and one way or another when Ramírez Berg and others mention how Rodriguez intermixes genres and conventions to *make new*, they are speaking about his creating this *enstrangement* in his viewers. This happens in additional ways. There is the use of Spanish with subtitles whereby English monolinguals will be forced to read the extraneous material at the bottom of the screen (subtitles), reminding them constantly of the artifice of the film. And there is the more organically integrated use of comic-book forms of *enstrangement*. So he presents the double of El Mariachi as a comic-book type that we identify as bad: bad guys are nearly always ugly in comic books. That is, their meanness is also embodied in their faces and bodies. Yet, the story is also a tragedy. Moco shoots a hole in El Mariachi's hand, he'll likely not be able to play guitar any longer; Domino dies and so too does El Mariachi's double, Azul — a character Rodriguez has us rooting for toward the end because he's not paid his due. Rodriguez *makes new* in the bringing together of philosophical meditation, the tragic, and the comic — comic book.

El Mariachi is conceived in terms of a generic approach — *narcotraficante* and adventure warrior, Leone Western and road movie, say — but Rodriguez complicates this generic approach with his infusion of the philosophical, the comical, and the tragic, with the doppelgänger and the comic-book sensibility. This is how he *makes new* and revitalizes our experience of the conventions of multiple genres.

We see with *El Mariachi* an approach to filmmaking that Rodriguez will follow even with larger budget movies. It's an approach whereby budget constraints can actually lead to innovation and creativity — to new ways of thinking about how to solve problems.

DESPERADO (1995)

O N AUGUST 25, 1995, RODRIGUEZ RELEASED THE SEC-
ond part in what would become identified later as his Mexico trilogy by critics — and as the title of the 2010-released DVD three-film box set. Now under the wing of Columbia Pictures, Rodriguez went from a budget of $7,000 to $7 million. He knew he could go large and make this small budget

relative to Hollywood action films look like a $50-million-plus summer block-buster. With some struggle not of his own making, he achieved the goal. The film brought in over $25 million at the box office.

The success of *El Mariachi* had led to its acquiring a solid identity of its own. So rather than remake *El Mariachi* with more money to throw at special effects, actors, and the like, this film would be a proper sequel. (Indeed, it was during this time that Tarantino suggested to Rodriguez that he make a third film in the series to make a Leone-like trilogy.) With his bigger budget he had access to more expensive film, editing, and sound equipment as well as a larger crew, including Guillermo Navarro, a Mexican DP (director of photography also for Guillermo Del Toro) with whom he would continue to work with on other films such as *Spy Kids*. He could cast professional actors, rising Hollywood stars at that. Rodriguez was eager to cast the charismatic Antonio Banderas (who had begun to cross over with *Philadelphia* and *Interview with the Vampire*), who could also sing and do his own stunts to take over the role from Carlos Gallardo, playing El Mariachi as emotionally jaded and willing to kill the drug lord, Bucho, played by Portuguese actor Joaquim de Almeida. After having seen *El Mariachi*, Banderas eagerly accepted the role. He cast the Mexican actress and telenovela star Salma Hayek to play the lead, the town's bookstore owner, Carolina, and Steve Buscemi as an American friend to El Mariachi and the storyteller who opens the film. He includes Latinos such as Cheech Marin as a bartender, Tito Larriva as a henchman, Tavo, and Danny Trejo as the assassin Navajas. Others like Tarantino (as the "Pick Up Guy") and Rodriguez's sisters and professional actresses Angela Lanza (as Tourist Girl), Patricia Vonne (Bar Girl), and Elizabeth Rodriguez (Mariachi Fan) make brief appearances as do the original *El Mariachi* actors Peter Marquardt (again as Moco) and Carlos Gallardo (now as the friend of El Mariachi, Campa). In each case, and knowing well the strengths and limitations of the actors, Rodriguez had already lined up the cast in his mind during the writing of the script.

Indeed, *Desperado* solidified the bankable screen presence of several of its actors: Salma Hayek would go on to star in *From Dusk till Dawn* (1996), Andy Tennant's *Fool's Rush In* (1997), and Barry Sonnenfeld's *Wild Wild West* (1999), among others, and Antonio Banderas would go on to have a blazing career playing in all genres, including action films such as *The Mask of Zorro* (1998) and its sequel as well as the more recent *Haywire* (2011). It also established the beginning of a trend Rodriguez would follow in subsequent films: a Leone approach to casting whereby he would use the same actors to play different roles in different films.

With access to Columbia Pictures' deeper pockets came many controlling stipulations—knots that Rodriguez found himself constantly trying to negotiate and untangle from. This began in preproduction with the studio's reticence in casting a Latina in the lead. They had in mind a blonde. Rodriguez had in mind—and had even written into the script—Salma Hayek. In anticipation of this, however, Rodriguez had cast her as the lead in the Showtime film *Roadracers*, which he made while waiting for Columbia to green-light *Desperado*. He also had her do a screen test with Banderas to show the studio the ready-made screen chemistry between the two. Rodriguez's foresight paid off. Columbia agreed to let him cast her, and she became the first Latina to play a lead in Hollywood since Dolores Del Río, née María de los Dolores Asúnsolo López-Negrete (1905–1938). To make life easier and knowing the topography well of Acuña, Mexico, Rodriguez wanted to shoot once again there; in fact, it was essential given that he could write a place he knew into the story, making the script more efficient for those he would have working on the film. The studio (and U.S. crew) didn't want the production to travel south of the border. As it turns out, this worked in Rodriguez's favor. He knew that having a local Mexican crew would generate a positive feeling among the people of Acuña and bring a positive energy to the production. That is, it would not appear to the locals that there was an invading mob of *gringos* coming to plunder the town and then leave.

While concessions were made, the studio didn't budge in other areas. For instance, they wouldn't give up their title. Rodriguez wanted *Pistolero*—a fitting title given that the story moves from one pistol shoot-out to another. To ensure a successful marketing to a non-Spanish-speaking mainstream, the studio insisted on *Desperado*—even though the film has little to do with the desperate, or desperate criminals. Rodriguez wanted to cut the film in Austin. The studio wanted him close by in LA. So he rented a house and filled it with editing and sound equipment where he and five sound editors (including two assistant editors) worked around the clock. In anticipation of this postproduction crunch, Rodriguez put together the music score (largely Los Lobos's *rock en español* and *ranchera* compositions) during the film's production. Not only would this save time in composing the actual score, but also in generating it during the shoot, it would fit more organically into the film as a whole; it would therefore also offer important cues to help make the editing of the film more efficient. (Notably, the story of *Desperado* takes place in the fictional town of Santa Cecilia, the patron saint of musicians; and Los Lobos's "Mariachi Suite" won the Grammy Award for Best Pop Instrumental Performance at the 1995 Grammy Awards.)

Given the relatively small budget for such a *big* film meant that Rodriguez had to work with a third of the time allotted to most action films; for what others would take four months to shoot, he had just over a month (thirty-nine days). While this was the kind of challenge Rodriguez liked to step up to, the largess of the production made this difficult. Producers visiting the set were unable to understand his way of filmmaking: shooting in ways that appeared to them to be haphazard, but that would become a completely coherent whole in postproduction. Rodriguez had already transformed the idea of the film into a full-cut story in his mind, so what might have appeared to be random was in fact very much controlled — allowing him to shoot scenes out of order, and that would save money. Rodriguez was uncomfortable *not* having as much control over the making of the film.

That said, he knew that if he didn't bring his so-called mariachi approach to the shoot, they would never wrap in time. He shot up to forty scenes a day. To save money, he learned in three days how to operate a Steadicam (saving the time also of explaining what he wanted to a third-party operator), he rented a crane for a few days from Texas for crane shots he knew would give it high production value, and when basic technology failed or was missing, he improvised; he strapped a camera to his shoulder while in a wheelchair to get his dolly shots, for instance. Knowing well that he would not be able to get all the filming done himself but unwilling to cede control to just anybody, he made the rather unconventional move of asking Antonio Banderas to direct the Second Unit crew; he knew that Banderas shared his vision of the film as a whole.

MAKING NEW

Because the film was known as a sequel to *El Mariachi* or by its generic convention (the warrior adventure and Western), Rodriguez could use the economy of form to take his audience somewhere at once familiar and different. The story picks up on the existential, lone-wanderer-cowboy quality that we end with in *El Mariachi*. The town where the action unfolds just happens to be a stop along the way of a never-ending journey. In this sense, we are very much in the generic domain of the Western. In yesteryear's Westerns such as *Bandido* (1956), *The Magnificent Seven* (1960), and *The Wild Bunch* (1969), for instance, Latinos appear as either passive, gullible peasants or gun-wielding *bandidos* and the Anglo cowboys as rational, savvy saviors; such films in toto come to represent, as Edward Buscombe identifies, "the clash between the traditional and the modern [and] the opposition of emotion and intellect" (23). Buscombe elaborates, writing how the United States is like the "seat of rational thought" and Mexico is the space of "raging passions" (23). Rodriguez seeks to turn this scenario right side up, creating Latino characters that are the subjects and agents of all that happens in the story.

Rodriguez adds several other ingredients, including the subduing of El Mariachi's drive to find work as a musician along with the simultaneous intensification of the impulse to protect innocents at any cost. Less mariachi and more

Desperado (1995). The American (Steve Buscemi) exaggerates facial
expressions when telling the bartender (Cheech Marín) of El Mariachi's
superheroic acts.

pistolero, El Mariachi states: "You know, it is easier to pull the trigger than play
the guitar, to destroy than to create." Rather than intensify this sensibility by
creating a doppelgänger theme seen in *El Mariachi*, Rodriguez throws the audience other metaphysical curve balls. First, he infuses El Mariachi with an overwhelming sense of the irony of his situation: in order to save the town's people
and their freedom to create (recall that the Mafioso Bucho blows up the town
bookstore, a repository of a collective imagination and, well, Carolina's stash of
cash that allows one the freedom from work in order to create), he must use
the power of the gun. As Mark Irwin writes, "The dramatic irony for the viewer
is that in participating in the mariachi's struggle for justice, it becomes possible
through the symbol of the gun to reappropriate the power of the guitar, whose
music dominates the soundtrack of both mariachi films" (77). Rodriguez complicates this further by creating a plot whereby El Mariachi discovers that his
archenemy Bucho is his brother. To return social balance and harmony to the
town, El Mariachi must sacrifice family.

Like *El Mariachi*, however, Rodriguez weaves into the film's weighty metaphysical and ethical threads the comical. He establishes this once again at the
outset of the story. The American (Buscemi) telling the bartender (Marin) the
extraordinary story of a larger-than-life El Mariachi shooting up a bar full of
goons is visually and aurally deliberately over the top. This not only creates the
epic dimension of the film, but it establishes Rodriguez's trademark comic-

book contract with the audience. We are to relish the heroic, epic dimension of what will unfold, but with a Tex Avery anything-goes attitude. Indeed, the choice of actors here is also appropriate. Buscemi's bug eyes and Marin's wide range of cartoon-like expressions further solidify the film's comic-book worldview. Rodriguez uses the camera and lighting to shape, reshape, and shape again Buscemi and Marin's already comic-book features. The techniques used in the opening storytelling sequence, with bad guys shot with such power that they blast into the air and the quick cuts that intensify our sensation and feeling of the action (sixteen cuts in one minute), not only make it look like a John Woo action film, but emphasize this Tex Avery cartoony worldview; in fact, exceptionally here with this opening sequence, to convey the feel and sense of the action he used his drawing skills to provide his crew and stuntmen a cartoon sketch for a storyboard.

In the visualizing and then making of the film's opening sequence, Rodriguez replaces his script with comic-book drawings; it enables the mental and emotional rehearsal of the scene in the crew; it allows for this to carry through the orchestration of the scene into the final product that will trigger a specific range of emotions and thoughts in the film-going audience. It's not therefore a simple replacement of the conventions of scripting or storyboarding without consequence. He uses video technology to preshoot footage as yet another means for exploring and then conveying this aesthetic and its cartoon-like sensibility.

Once we are in the storyworld, we see that Rodriguez continues to combine elements of the heroic and comic, the serious with the comic-book sensibility; much of the action breaks all sorts of basic law-like structures that govern the universe, including gravity. It is within this storyworld that audiences can at once immerse themselves in the comic-book anything-goes sense of things and experience a critique of the kinds of exploitation seen when capitalism has devolved to its most barbaric form: the murder, exploitation, and oppression of drug-lording.

Rodriguez's struggle with Columbia Pictures came to an end once he wrapped *Desperado* and was out of his two-year contract with them. He was already back having fun making "The Misbehavers" and beginning the preproduction for *From Dusk till Dawn*. When he signed on with the next studio, the Weinstein Brothers' Miramax/Dimension, he was able to negotiate a contract that gave him total artistic control over his films as well as the freedom to live and work from his home in Austin.

*I*T WOULD BE A NUMBER OF YEARS AND FOUR OR SO FILMS later before Rodriguez would be able to get to the third installment of what Tarantino (on the set of *Desperado*) called his version of Sergio Leone's Dollar Trilogy. (Leone's Dollar Trilogy was made up of his 1964 *A Fistful of Dollars*, the 1965 *For a Few Dollars More*, and a year later, his *The Good, the Bad and the Ugly*.) James J. Donahue considers how this third film in the Mariachi trilogy continues to turn upside down the stereotypical representation of *el mariachi* as a "cross-genre signifier for American film audiences" of Mexico as a source of entertainment. Rather, in this film we see the figure of the mariachi portrayed as a "developing character-gunslinger" (forthcoming). For Donahue, he develops from a loner character in the first film, *El Mariachi*, to an "integral part of a larger social unit" in this final film in the trilogy.

To take advantage of (and possibly avoid conflicts with) an impending log-jam with the Screen Actors Guild strike that would free up the time of certain A-list actors, Rodriguez wrote the screenplay in two weeks to be able to move swiftly into production. He knew there would be a small window of opportunity for actors like Banderas to be available for the shoot. The strike also imposed certain time limits on the production — the kind of high-pressure-cooker environment Rodriguez seems to thrive in.

His budget and access to A-list actors brought the shoot to seven weeks. After two weeks of preparation, he began shooting on *Once Upon a Time in Mexico* in and around San Miguel de Allende and Guanajuato, Mexico, in May 2001. (He had found the area when scouting for *Zorro* — a film he dropped due to budget disagreements with Tri-Star.) As on the other two films, most of his crew was Mexican. While he managed to get his all-star cast and shot the film swiftly, its postproduction would be delayed somewhat by the need to shoot, score, edit, and release *Spy Kids 2: The Island of Lost Dreams*; to help finance *Spy Kids 2*, he cut a deal with McDonald's that locked him into a specific release date. And, to save time and cost, during this period he also made *Spy Kids 3-D: Game Over*.

With domestic distribution by Columbia Pictures (and its international distribution with Dimension Films), on September 12, 2003, *Once Upon a Time* hit 3,282 theaters domestically. It opened at the No. 1 Box Office spot, making $23.4 million the opening weekend. It went on to gross over $56.3 million domestically and an additional $41.8 million worldwide.

That this was "A Robert Rodriguez Flick" (announced thus in the opening credits) was a guarantee of high-octane action and entertainment. It was also the first high-budget feature film shot with HD technology. All this, including an all-star cast, seemed a guarantee of its success. The cast includes Antonio Banderas (El Mariachi), Salma Hayek (love interest Carolina), Eva Mendes (AFN operative Ajedrez), Johnny Depp (CIA agent Sheldon Sands), Willem Dafoe (the archvillain Armando Barillo), Mickey Rourke (as American fugitive Billy Chambers), Mexico's Pedro Armendáriz Jr. (President of Mexico), Rubén Blades (as FBI agent Jorge Ramírez), Danny Trejo (as the knife-throwing henchman, Cucuy) — even the heartthrob and pop singer Enrique Iglesias (as El Mariachi's friend, Lorenzo).

As we would expect of a "Robert Rodriguez Flick," it was also a training ground of sorts. After George Lucas introduced HD technology to Rodriguez in January 2000, he knew he could never go back to regular film. He screen-tested the quality of regular film stock against HD (Sony's HDW-F900 HDCAM CineAlta 24P), realizing that it offered more possibilities and greater control over the final product. He liked its light weight and smooth-zoom capabilities and the ability to see the shot instantaneously (as opposed to waiting for dailies). He knew that this would offer him more freedom to push the film-making envelope. To become adept at this new technology, he bought two Sony HDW-F900 cameras with a wide range of Fujinon and Angenieux lenses. He used this equipment to shoot *Once Upon a Time* and then *Spy Kids 2*. With video engineers on standby, he was able to customize the cameras to come up with a wide range of unique looks in the film. In an interview for Brian McKernan and Bob Zahn he remarks: "HD is very freeing and is more like going back to the basics of filmmaking, where it's fun again. It's just so much easier to shoot in HD. I was able to light and even DP myself because I was able to see what I was getting on my monitors and be much edgier with the lighting because I knew I wasn't going to get into trouble; there was no guesswork or waiting for dailies" (28).

Working with HD also allowed Rodriguez to save time and therefore money on the shoot. He could do all the special effects in postproduction — from bullets riddling church walls to Depp's hollowed-out eye sockets or digitally erasing crane and wires on the set — that enabled him to keep to the same production schedule of *Desperado*, but with many more effects. *Once Upon a Time* was budgeted for 70 and yet ended up with 400 effects shots, but because of the HD technology, Rodriguez was able to stay under budget. (And he was rather ahead of the curve here; today digital filmmaking is so prevalent that several of the major companies that made 35mm cameras no longer do so.)

HD also allowed him a certain freedom and efficiency when it came to cutting and scoring the film. He cut the film digitally on a series of networked Avid Media Composer and Unity systems. He scored the film digitally as well; with a music keyboard, hooked to a computer equipped with software synthesizers and music programs, he could isolate the layers of sound (punches and gunfire from dialogue, as well as drums, strings, and other instrument sounds in the music score, for instance) that he could move around and synch up in precise ways during postproduction.

This technology came at a good moment. He had run into union (Austin Federation of Musicians) issues with the Austin Symphony; he wanted to contract with them to do some nonunion recording sessions to keep costs down (distributors Sony and Dimension/Miramax dislike adding aftermarket payments to their overall budget) and promised that *Spy Kids 3-D* would be done under union contract, as had been done with *Spy Kids 2*. So he scored the film himself and included compositions by his band Chingon such as "Cuka Rocka."

Knowing well that creativity doesn't come from divine inspiration and that it develops importantly in cooperative work, he invited some of his actors who were also musicians such as Johnny Depp, Banderas, and Blades to come up with musical motifs for their characters. He would use the collaboratively constructed sound design to integrate all the parts of the film.

Rodriguez retrained himself to become one of the first filmmakers to use HD cameras. In this he succeeded. The film he trained on was a commercial success. Its success, however, didn't quite match up to its critical reception. As Alison Macor sums up, "Although many critics were impressed by Rodriguez's growing list of talents and his ability to make digital virtually indistinguishable from film, they were less enamored by his narrative abilities" (290–291). More pointed criticisms included Kim Newman's for *Sight & Sound*. The fragmented multiple plotlines that don't seem to cohere lead Newman to ask if the protagonist is given much of a narrative at all (59). For Newman, the best moments are indeed the most coherent and fleshed-out story threads such as the flashbacks, or story within the story, of the time Carolina (Salma Hayek) and El Mariachi adventure together (in a dramatic escape scene, shackled together, they cascade down the side of a hotel building) before her untimely murder; however, even this thread is left untied, making it feel, according to Newman, like "chunks of an abandoned Mariachi movie" (59). She concludes, "He remains a busy, inventive filmmaker, but here [. . .] the character focus that made earlier installments more than genre tossoffs has been lost in pursuit of cramming the screen with *stuff*" (59).

No artist is above critique. Rodriguez does include multiple plotlines — many of which *do not* tie up nicely. It is a story filled with conspiracy threads such as drug baron Armando Barillo's paying General Emiliano Marquez (Gerardo Vigil) to plot a coup against the president of Mexico. It includes all kinds of characters from the vengeful to the lustful to the greedy and sociopathic. It includes romance, revenge, double- and triple-crossed betrayal, and governmental corruption plots. Here we ask, as Newman and others before, where is the clear-cut vision of the goals that Rodriguez set himself? What is actually the story line in film? Does the film succeed? Do we fault the film for not providing enough context concerning the workings of Mexico's executive, legislative, parliamentary, and judicial power structures? Does the film actually reveal anything in terms of real identifiable corruption and degree of penetration of drug money at all levels of the state apparatus?

Some of the stunts and acting give the feeling of déjà vu. We ask ourselves, have we not already seen this in *Desperado* or in other action films? It is the accumulation of feelings of déjà vu that threaten to create a sense of habituation in the audience. And, one might suppose, as Newman does, that the story line lacks complexity, or thickness. The El Mariachi character appears — and now with two new sidekicks, but we don't know what they are doing and why they are doing it. We might ask these questions: What are their motivations for joining El Mariachi and his crusade to avenge the murder of his wife and daughter? Why does the film end with El Mariachi wearing the Mexican flag? Was it his patriotism that led him to risk his life?

However, what Rodriguez makes clear in the opening credits, that this is a "flick" "Shot, chopped and scored by Robert Rodriguez," lends support to the fact that these are deliberate slips. It's a story that includes anything and everything, including fake arms and eviscerated eyes. Its characters speak pearls and also comical lines like Sands asking Cucuy: "Are you a Mexi*can* or a Mexi*cant*?" It includes the romance, revenge, and so on plotlines that don't wrap well, but perhaps they don't need to. Perhaps all this is another iteration of the comic-book sensibility that allows for the inclusion of an otherwise unlikely high-noon-styled showdown where a bloodied orbital-socket agent Sands shoots bad guys — not by sight, but by sound. That is, like a Leone film, *Once Upon a Time in Mexico* asks its audience to step into the cartoon mode: to enjoy and not take it too seriously.

SPAGHETTI REBOOT

To do so, the audience needs to work from a context: the career film-maker Rodriguez's comic-book sensibility and the spaghetti western (filmed in Italy and Spain) or the tortilla western (filmed in Mexico) of the 1960s and 1970s. Characterized by its move away from good vs. bad contrasts of the American Western, these films presented morally ambiguous, self-serving protagonists and antagonists alike. Some scholars consider how these films explore critically or uncritically the class conflict, themes of wealth and violence — and, of course, race, gender, and sexuality. Others consider how spaghetti westerns are reflective of an epoch of little hope and much transition. As Patrick McGee deduces from the films of the progenitor of this genre, Sergio Leone, "There are no true heroes in Leone's world, only men who have lost all hope and yet discipline themselves to perform acts of the will driven by vengeance, greed, or simply the inexplicable desire to prevent a strong person from exploiting a weaker one. Their motives are usually mixed, and Leone seems to imply that anything good can only come from a willingness to risk the possibility of doing something evil" (168). For McGee, *Once Upon a Time in the West* most clearly represents this epoch's simultaneous pessimism and hope; it "expresses a negative and almost elegiac view of everything that will be lost in the process of creating a new and potentially more just world" (180). (For a detailed and exhaustive breakdown of the spaghetti western as a genre see Frayling; Fridlund; Hughes.)

Perhaps it is not so surprising, then, that Rodriguez should choose to bring his comic-book worldview to bear on his rebooting and revamping of the spaghetti western. Indeed, directors such as Damiano Damiani, Sergio Sollima, and Sergio Corbucci used the spaghetti format to overturn expectation and set up opposition between an outsider (Europe or the United States) and indigenous revolutionaries—all while entertaining the audience. It is here that Rodriguez can continue to position Latinos as positively valued protagonists (El Mariachi) of the action and Anglos as negatively valued (Sands). As already mentioned, Edward Buscombe considers how Rodriguez complicates the typical representation of U.S. characters as rational with those of Mexico as excessively emotional. This is especially visible in Rodriguez's collapsing the worldviews of Sands (United States) with Barillo (Mexico). For Buscombe, they are "united in their single-minded pursuit of money" (24).

Buscombe carefully identifies the parallels between Rodriguez and Leone:

> His film is essentially a collection of action sequences, fast paced and skillfully choreographed, shot and edited (Rodriguez is his own cameraman and editor); the frequent use of the zoom lens gives the film a curiously authentic 1960s feel. The music, also composed by Rodriguez, is a straight pastiche of Ennio Morricone. A Leone trademark is the longdrawn-out, elaborately staged showdown between two gunfighters, in which all attempt at realism is abandoned and the action slowed to a seemingly endless series of close-ups. (24)

And a Leone trademark also includes "outre weaponry" like a flame-thrower gun snapping out of a guitar case. Buscombe, however, comments that Rodriguez sacrifices his "narrative plausibility" to convey a stylized world where a shot and blinded Sands with his pair of six-guns is more baroque aesthetic artifact than action hero. For Buscombe, the violence is "pretty" but without consequence (24).

Do we go to the film for those answers I posed earlier regarding the interlacing of government and drug money? Or do we go for the reasons we might watch a spaghetti western or a Tex Avery cartoon: To revel in the impossibility of the action of the characters. With this in mind and fully accepting the contract Rodriguez asks us to sign here, I wonder if this film evinces a clear-cut vision or idea of the goals that Rodriguez set himself? One has the sense that Rodriguez's having a clear sense of the film — cutting the film in his head before production begins — gives way to the sense that there was too much scripting on the fly.

Until rather recently, because the old cameras were so cumbersome, the time actors had to wait between one shot and another was very long; it could take several hours to set up the next shot. Making films could be very tedious for actors — and the many working on the set. Making a film could take months and months. As I mentioned, this is what drove Kazan from the business. So it is true that an excessive slowness in filming can work against creativity, including that of the actors. It is also true that advances in technology have put cameras in the hands of those like Rodriguez; and with HD, he can have even more control over the making of the film and therefore more carefully guide how it will trigger new sensations, thoughts, and feelings in the audience. In the hands of another, rapidity might be an enemy of creativity. If a director doesn't have clearly in mind what he or she wants as well as know how to obtain the results (and have the requisite skill), it can be the death of creativity.

This is why in the last instance we need to keep in mind chronology. *Once Upon a Time* was an exercise in learning HD filmmaking. It was also a commercial success. However, in terms of an aesthetic whole, it is not the best of the three that make up the trilogy. With his subsequent films, as he has a better command of HD, the technology becomes more and more a servant to his creativity and he can be more effective and more conscious of aesthetic goals and means as aesthetics, and not just as technology. This might be a case where Rodriguez makes a film to master a new technology (HD) but where the new technology has yet to become handmaiden to the shaping of the story.

Regenerative Aesthetics of Degenerate Genres

FROM DUSK TILL DAWN (1996)

FRESH OFF THE MAKING OF *DESPERADO*, RODRIGUEZ turned his focus back to a story that had caught his attention: Tarantino's script about psychopath fugitives running from the law and Mexican vampires. Tarantino had Rodriguez in mind when writing the script—and Rodriguez wanted to make the film. Since the making of his vignette "The Misbehavers" (*Four Rooms*) and spending time together on *Desperado*, like two kids in a sandbox, Rodriguez's friendship with Tarantino grew. He wanted Tarantino for the role of one of the brothers, Richie Gecko, in *From Dusk till Dawn* and for Tarantino to be around as much as possible in the making of the film.

Being free from Columbia Pictures breathing down his back did not mean that Rodriguez's frustrations were over. He was working with a larger budget ($20 million) than for *Desperado* and had Miramax involved in the production. This meant that he would still face certain challenges and obstacles interfering with his work; he felt like a hired hand and *not* the director of the film.

Miramax was not familiar with how Rodriguez worked—that he had a total sense of the whole film (shots, angles, edits, sound design) in his mind before production would begin. This was a problem Rodriguez would soon solve once his in-house producer Elizabeth Avellán came on board with his other films. (Rodriguez could not have the entire film shot in his head because Tarantino deliberately kept out the script's final three pages; however, he assured Rodriguez that they would know how to end the film once in production. He did know how to end it: with an iconoclastic image of an ancient Aztec–Mayan temple descending into a cavernous pit.) And, because they were higher profile than most independent films (given the Tarantino and Rodriguez names and a bigger budget than most indies have) the IATSE (International Alliance of Theatrical Stage Employees) made gestures toward shutting down the production. Tensions arose between executive producers (Lawrence Bender and Tarantino) and coproducers (Paul Hellerman and Avellán) as well as Rodriguez and the unions. Attempts were made to connect with union organizer Lyle Trachtenberg of the IATSE, but to no avail. (See the short documentary "Full Tilt Boogie" included as part of the DVD set of *From Dusk till Dawn*.) While nothing materialized, this laid a heavy blanket of anxiety over the production.

Curveballs aside, Rodriguez could get into his sandbox and begin to make his genre mash-up movie magic. After reading the script, Rodriguez knew who he wanted to be in on the making of the film. With Tarantino having developed a good working relationship with Harvey Keitel in *Reservoir Dogs* and *Pulp Fiction*, as well as George Clooney when directing episodes of *ER*, Rodriguez was able to line up an A-grade list of actors — to star in what would be considered a film in the exploitation (crime/vampire) B-film mode. As Seth Gecko, Clooney's good looks and dominant personality would balance out the more violent and sociopathic characterization of the brother, Richie (Tarantino). (Not only did Clooney pick up a couple of acting awards for his role, including MTV Best Breakthrough Performance, but this was Clooney's first cross-over into film, showcasing his bankability to Hollywood execs.) Rodriguez had in mind Salma Hayek in the role of the queen vampire, Satánico Pandemónium. There could be no other actress for this part. Keitel would play the role of the pastor with Juliette Lewis as his daughter, Kate. Latinos appear in such roles as Danny Trejo as the bartender Razor Charlie (he appears in all three iterations of *From Dusk*), Tito Larriva (also in *Desperado*) as a band member playing at the Titty Twister, and Cheech Marin in three roles as U.S./Mexico border patrol, Chet Pussy, and the gangster Carlos. Actors affiliated with the B-film industry such as Tom Savini and Fred Williamson appear, respectively, as a crotch-pistol-flipping biker and a Vietnam vet.

Having worked with DP Guillermo Navarro (*Desperado* and "The Misbehavers"), Rodriguez brought him on board to share in the camera work. Rodriguez would also use the Steadicam-operator skills that he had mastered when making *Desperado*. Another familiar face from *Desperado* he brought on board was Ethan Maniquis (editor of the award-winning Venezuelan film *Sequestro Express*) as assistant editor. He knew Maniquis from his apprentice editor work on *Four Rooms*. (Maniquis would become associate editor on *Once Upon a Time in Mexico* and then editor on *Shorts* and *Planet Terror*; he would go on to codirect *Machete* with Rodriguez.) The music score would include ZZ Top, Stevie Ray Vaughan, and Jimmie Vaughan for the honky-tonk and blues-rock feel of the first half of the film; and music by the Blasters and Tito Larriva would establish the horror/rock feel of the second half.

Knowing that this would be his first no-holds-barred venture into exploitation, drive-in, B-genre filmmaking, Rodriguez shot, cut, and scored *From Dusk till Dawn*. Miramax/Dimension released *From Dusk till Dawn* on January 19, 1996. Whether because of the time of year or because of its release to an audience unprepared for a film that revels in its own exploitation experience, the film didn't do well. Recall that by the mid-1990s, Hollywood was making watered down horror films in the hopes of attracting, mainstream otherwise nonhorror-genre-seeking audiences. The film brought in a little more than its cost to make: $25 million. The critics were also less than excited. The mainstream critical reviews ranged from being critical of its violence and nihilist attitude to its being too self-satisfied about its hipster attitude; oddly, some critics considered it humdrum.

From Dusk till Dawn did do well enough in its afterlife as a video, prompting Rodriguez along with Tarantino and Lawrence Bender, who also produced *Four Rooms*, to serve as producers in the making of two more direct-to-video films in the series: *Texas Blood Money* (with Robert Patrick, an actor Rodriguez would use in *The Faculty*) follows chronologically as a sequel to the first, and *The Hangman's Daughter* works as a prequel to the first that takes the story (screenplay by Alvaro Rodriguez from a story by Robert and Alvaro Rodriguez) back to a late nineteenth-century U.S./Mexico borderlands setting.

CRIMESPLOITATION

In many ways the film is a Tarantino and Rodriguez product. As Mark Irwin observes, the first section is "modeled after 'psychopulp' masters like Jim Thompson and Charles Willeford, and is the kind of loquacious crime film we have come to expect from Tarantino" (72). The second section is more "typical of Rodriguez's visually oriented style of fast cuts and unusual angles, is an homage to 1970s drive-in classics like John Carpenter's *Assault on Precinct 13* and George Romero's *Dawn of the Dead*" (72).

Let me break this down even further. Long before the end credits roll (he thanks pulp novelist Jim Thompson here), Rodriguez lays out the filmic contract with his audience. The film's opening sequence (the first nine minutes) establishes this. It opens with a crane shot of a nondescript, square-shaped 1970s-styled brown American-made sedan traveling down a wide stretch of empty road; the landscape is arid and big sky wide open. Without the audience's knowing exactly where this is, from the landscape we know that it's somewhere in the Southwest. (This is confirmed shortly after with "Texas" postcards appearing in a rack at the gas station.) The car pulls into a gas station. The sign on top of the building reads: Benny's: World of Liquor. The camera cuts to actor

Michael Parks as Earl McGraw getting out of this car with a holstered gun and cowboy hat; Rodriguez cast him here and in *Planet Terror* (Tarantino in *Kill Bill* and *Death Proof*) because of his distinctively Anglo-cowboy-like drawl and exaggerated Texan-cowboy-like mannerisms. We hear wind rustling and the police radio squelch as he struts into Benny's. Inside, he converses with a caricature of a gas station attendant, an exaggerated gesturing and talking Pete (played by John Hawkes from *Roadracers*).

While the film already begins to visually set up comic-book sensibility, it also insists that we hang any political correctness at the door: Earl complains to Pete about a variously identified "mongoloid," "retard," or "potato head" working at the local diner. Pete replies, "That boy belongs under a circus tent, not flipping burgers." Two men appear out of the shadows, dragging two young women with them and holding guns to their heads; violent, frenzied movement along with exaggerated expressions of fear (Pete and the young women, especially) take place as a slowly building ominous sound enters the extradiegetic auditory channel.

In a one-take shot, Rodriguez shows bullets flying, blood splattering, corpses piling up—Pete's body rising and then falling up in a ball of flames as he dies popping popcorn with the heat of his body. He concludes the scene with a shot of the Gecko brothers walking away from the carnage. The gas station blows. The opening credits roll, and honky-tonk music and muffler rumble fill the sound space. We see the Gecko brothers' dusty Mercury Cougar XR-7 drive down the road. As it pulls away to the left of the frame, in the blink of an eye, Rodriguez's special effects have us seeing with Superman's x-ray vision a woman tied up in the trunk of the car. Rodriguez (with Tarantino's script) squarely lands the audience in the exploitation *and* comic-book film storytelling world.

Once the story proper begins, Rodriguez reminds us constantly of the film's worldview. While waiting for Seth to return to the motel with something to eat (in an intertextual nod to *Pulp* he does so with the fictional Kahuna Burgers franchise), Richie channel surfs; with each click we see a glimpse of a cartoon (Tex Avery?), Kubrick's sacrificial epic *Spartacus*, and then a Western. And, moving into super exploitation mode, Richie rapes and brutally murders the kidnapped woman (Brenda Hillhouse), who we learn was a bank teller from an earlier bank robbery and rampage. Throughout, Rodriguez intersperses the deep ominous rumble heard earlier. Those who understood the film's raison d'être and signed the contract accordingly would be able to understand, even if not stated as such, that Rodriguez aimed to create an aesthetic relationship between his audience and the story. Members of the MPAA rating board clued into its over-the-top spirit, agreeing to give it an R—and not an unratable rating. (Notably, when there is more blood splattering in the latter part of the

From Dusk till Dawn *(1996). X-ray vision camera trick used to show tied-up bank clerk in the trunk of Gecko brothers' Mercury Cougar XR-7.*

film, it is mostly green, vampire blood. The MPAA doesn't like to see too much red.) And critic Marc Savlov gets it, writing "Fans of Merchant–Ivory will do well to steer clear of Rodriguez's newest opus, but both action and horror film fans have cause for celebration after what seems like a particularly long splatter-drought. This is horror with a wink and a nod to drive-in theatres and sweaty back seats. This is how it's done." Those critics who missed these cues, however, read Richie's psychopathic behavior too straight-faced, rejecting the film for its violence.

MONSTERSPLOITATION

Already in the first part of the film, we see the triggering of seeming incongruent emotions: fear with laughter, repulsion, and attraction. We see this also in the pairing of the brothers: one repulsive in behavior (Tarantino) and the other handsome in looks (Clooney). The repulsive and attractive are inseparable. Conjoined like Siamese twins, with few exceptions the brothers are always together. The one time they are apart, Richie brutally rapes and murders, causing Seth concern, but never separation.

This conjoining of beauty and ugly intensifies as they cross the border into Mexico. The border patrol officer (Cheech Marin) searches Pastor Jacob Fuller's (Keitel) Pace Arrow RV, narrowly missing sight of the stowed-away Gecko brothers; earlier they had taken hostage the pastor, his daughter Kate (Lewis), and Scott (Ernest Liu), realizing that hiding in the RV would be the way to cross the border without police detection. The border patrol officer passes them through to Mexico. Forty-one minutes into the film Rodriguez lays the groundwork for the audience to regear its generic expectation: from on-the-lam, kidnap, psycho-gangster flick to south-of-the-border vamp-thriller. At night, the Pace Arrow RV arrives at the Titty Twister bar and strip club. At the door appears Chet Pussy (Cheech Marin once again, but with bushy black eyebrows and goatee) announcing,

> Pussy, pussy, pussy! All pussy must go. At the Titty Twister we're slashing pussy in half! This is a pussy blow out! Make us an offer on our vast selection of pussy! We got white pussy, black pussy, Spanish pussy, yellow pussy, hot pussy, cold pussy, wet pussy, tight pussy, big pussy, bloody pussy, fat pussy, hairy pussy, smelly pussy, velvet pussy, silk pussy, Naugahyde pussy, snappin' pussy, horse pussy, dog pussy, mule pussy, fake pussy! If we don't have it, you don't want it!

The encyclopedic laundry list of types of "pussy" together with Marin's appearing as yet another cartoon-styled character remind us once again of the aesthetic relation that Rodriguez aims for here: the irreverence of the carnivalesque, a storytelling mode that asks the audience to revel in the corporeal (in both its beautiful and ugly manifestations) and that suspends ethical judgment (prudish and high-minded especially). The carnivalesque as ingredient in the grotesque is a familial kin to the gothic storytelling mode that, as described by Ruth Helyer, provokes "fear and fascination" (725) and where the "monstrous undead, present us with 'doubles,' the other side to the traits respectable society has chosen to uphold" (726).

This carnivalesque mode has been present, of course, since the dawn of storytelling, especially coming into its own in the literary arts with sixteenth-century author François Rabelais's *Gargantua and Pantagruel*. Recall, too, Rabelais's love of the laundry lists that would be so long and detailed they would inevitably move readers to laughter. He uses exact figures — 384 pigs, 1,001 horses, and all figures exaggerated but precise, including the invention of Pantagruel and Gargantua. From beginning to end, the novel is a systematic application of the aesthetic of the grotesque. It is also the prevalent storytelling mode that informs Mexico's El Santo films with the famed luchador battling space aliens, vampires, and all variety of other monsters. It is the sensibility that José Majica Marins (a.k.a. "Coffin Joe") brings to his Brazilian-made and set crazy gorefest flicks. (For more on this, see Newitz's "What Makes Things Cheesy?") It is within the conventions of the Italian vampire ("spaghetti nightmare") exploitation films made popular by Dario Argento, Lucio Fulci, or Mario Bava. Films that, as Dana Renga discusses, use themes of apocalypse, threats of immigrant influx, or terrorism to "*exploit* the viewer can provide some sort of catharsis through identification with a persecuted hero/protagonist" (245). It is the kind

From Dusk till Dawn (1996). Salma Hayek as Satánico
Pandemónium.

of film that caters to a pizza-eating, beer-imbibing U.S. *Fangoria* crowd who
seek pleasure out in the encounter with excess, who seek out films that are not
afraid to flaunt the excess of their own horror.

The Titty Twister is the conjoining of contrasts as part of the carnivalesque —
a central ingredient of the grotesque. Cheech Marin's playful incantation of
pussy contrasting with his ugly manners and presence fits well with the Titty
Twister's own baroque interior architecture that is appealing yet at the same
time not exactly beautiful; the slithering half-naked beautiful bodies of the
women are set against a sea of brutish, macho-animalistic males — of course,
even this is done with great playfulness, especially noticeable when Sex Machine (Tom Savini) shows off a pistol that flips from a cod piece on his crotch.

Fifty-five minutes into the film, Rodriguez introduces the audience to the
pure embodiment of the aesthetics of the grotesque. Razor Charlie (Trejo)
introduces Satánico Pandemónium, and a bikini-clad Salma Hayek appears
on the stage wearing scarf-like around her shoulders a slithering albino snake.
Rodriguez choreographs her movement and body in such a way that creates in
her audience (and us as film-going audience by proxy) an intense relationship
between her beauty and the repulsiveness of the python. She morphs into an
ugly creature yet still retains a beautiful body. She is a mixture of the beautiful
and the ugly. Rodriguez asks that we contemplate her in this moment of transformation from beautiful to ugly, evoking a deep sense of beauty in her body as
well as a horror and disgust in her transmogrification. He reminds us that the
ugly can be found in nature; it can create a certain relation to the viewer, and this
can be sometimes captured, as Rodriguez does, in its artistic reconstruction.

The sight of Richie's hand dripping with blood transforms Hayek from beautiful to a combination of the beautiful and the ugly — or the grotesque. Blood-
thirsty, her hybrid self appears as her head transforms into a scaly reptile head
that bites into Richie; her body remains that of a woman. To trigger in the audi-

From Dusk till Dawn *(1996)*. *Salma Hayek transforms from the beautiful to the repulsive.*

ence a sense of this double feeling of repulsion and attraction when she shape-shifts into the grotesque, we hear her growl and the music shifts from the Tito & Tarantula *rock en español* ("Angry Cockroaches") playing earlier in the scene to an ominous sound conventionally associated with horror films. The music together with the ever proliferating bodily transformation of humans into monsters—all variety of horrible-looking hybrid human/monster creatures—underline and intensify the grotesque and our relationship with the grotesque: the hybrid presence of the beautiful and the ugly.

BORDERLANDS

With the closing shot—after a disco ball kills all the monsters not as death of disco, but death of monsters—Rodriguez pans out from the back-side of the Titty Twister and we see that in fact it is the tip of an ancient Mayan temple that descends into a pit of wrecked trucks and bikes; the waste presumably of all the truckers and bikers left behind by truckers and bikers. Rodriguez thus also inscribes the film, and with a big ironic wink, into a tradition of films that, as Camilla Fojas writes, depict "the U.S.–Mexico border as a lawless place ruled by a dark mythology, and home to every illicit activity and industry" (183). Fojas continues, "Hollywood border films have always been primarily about the maintenance of the integrity of U.S. national identity and the need to control the border to exclude foreign-born populations" (183). She considers Holly-wood border films such as Welles's *Touch of Evil* (1958), *The Border* (1982), *Traffic*

(2000), and *Kingpin* (NBC, 2003), among others, as revealing an underside to drugs and/or bodies crossing over, a fear of an invasion of Brown-others from the south.

Rodriguez wanted to make this exploitation pulp/horror/vamp film *Latino*. With the last pages of the Tarantino script left a blank slate, and already building on the research done on Mayan–Aztec monster lore, to conclude the film, in postproduction he added the visual effects shot of a Mayan–Aztec temple (the painting of which still hangs high and large in the main conference area of Troublemaker Studios). Rodriguez's grotesque, then, is also a borderland that upends the tradition of the border narrative. He reverses, to use Fojas's terminology, the "focalization on the part of protagonists" (193), asking his audience to disidentify with the main Anglo characters (psychopaths) and to appreciate, think, and feel for the Latinos in more complex, hybrid ways.

REPULSIVE/ATTRACTIVE CONJOINED

By combining with exploitation/pulp genre, Rodriguez makes new our experience of film. He couldn't exist as a filmmaker if he didn't have systematic recourse to the grotesque. Rodriguez creates a film whereby there is a seamless mixture (fusion) of beauty and ugliness permanently present in the aesthetics of the film. But there is more.

Throughout the film we feel the influence of Tarantino. He wrote the screenplay. He's also attracted toward the grotesque, but with a more realistic-oriented aesthetics. Whether in his early film *Pulp Fiction* (1994) or his screenplay for *Natural Born Killers* (1994) we see in Tarantino's work the saturation of violence. He achieved his effects in the accumulation of violence as per a realist aesthetics. That is, Tarantino arrives at the grotesque by the accumulation of ultrarealistic violence. The grotesque is the peak, or summa, of the accumulation of violence. It is the climax as a kind of side product of the accumulation of violence. This is certainly why the first part of the film is also played in terms of the coalescing of repulsive and attractive dualities in the more realist identifiable psychopathology of the Gecko brothers.

However, the constant aesthetic we see in Rodriguez is a completely different aesthetic: it's through and through the aesthetic of the grotesque. Beginning with his earliest films, he already practiced the aesthetic of the grotesque. This aesthetic guides all his films. He begins his film career with the grotesque—the fusion of the ugly/beautiful for a unified aesthetic affect—and applies this aesthetic to all of his subsequent films.

Indeed, we might even consider *From Dusk till Dawn* an admixture of two different approaches to the aesthetic of the grotesque. From the moment the

RV arrives at the Titty Twister, we are almost totally in the Rodriguez aesthetic—one that follows a Tex Avery comic–like sensibility in its composition and content: from the way Cheech as Chet Pussy entices clients to the Titty Twister to the crotch-pistol to Hayek's transmogrification. It is the mention of Chango—a Chango poster appears in *The Faculty* and in *Spy Kids* as well as the name of beer served in *Desperado*. (Chango as in monkey that calls to mind the playful and mischievous; it might tangentially also call to mind Changó the rascal deity of the Afro-Hispanic Caribbean who plays tricks to avenge crimes against the innocent.) It is upon arrival at the Titty Twister where we see Rodriguez's grotesque sensibility come into its own as the operating principle in content and form.

THE FACULTY (1998)

*I*N 1997 THE WEINSTEIN BROTHERS APPROACHED RODRIguez. They knew he could put a stop to the potential money hemorrhage that was otherwise about to happen with the production of Kevin Williamson's (of *Scream 1* and *2*) sci-fi/horror teen script, *The Faculty*. They were also worried about the teen-horror-flick genre losing momentum at the box office. The stakes were high, of course. This was not the way Rodriguez liked to work; it was not his script and he would be working as a hired hand of sorts. So in return the Weinstein brothers offered him a "five-picture deal in addition to the overall deal Rodriguez had first made with the company in May 1995" (Macor 275). Rodriguez agreed to take it on, but he would be its editor and Avellán would be producer (along with the Weinsteins). It would also have to be filmed in and around Austin—not only to save Miramax money, but so Rodriguez could be close to family and so he could put together and acclimate a film production crew to his method and approach.

With a $15 million budget, Rodriguez began production that spring, shooting primarily in and around Austin. A leased warehouse, an abandoned building at the Texas School for the Deaf, and the nearby Lockhart High School served as sets to what would became the fictional Herrington High School in a fictional town in Ohio. Putting the crew through a demanding shooting schedule made it difficult for some like the DP and visual effects crew. Nonetheless, Rodriguez wrapped the production in July. However, following the success of *Scream*'s release on Christmas Day the year before, the Weinstein brothers decided to release *The Faculty* on December 25, 1998. It opened on 2,365 screens in the United States, pulling in over \$11.8 million on its opening weekend. While it would go on to gross over \$40.2 million domestically, it didn't do as well as anticipated. The industry seemed to know this was the fault of Williamson — and not Rodriguez.

The film opens first with the sound of an electric guitar strumming an identifiable rock tune: The Offspring's "The Kids Aren't Alright" (about suburbia/small town swallowing up lives of youth). This is followed by a shot of a football flying through the air, voices saying "Look out," and the sound of the thump of the ball as it's caught by a footballer. The camera pulls back for the audience to see a bunch of large-bodied, maroon, yellow, and gray clad football players pushing chaotically against each other on the field, and a whistle sounds. Cut to the coach (whom the audience might recognize as Robert Patrick from the 1991 *Terminator 2*) throwing down his game plan in a tempestuous fit: "God damn it. You call that blocking, you bunch of jokes!" The camera then cuts to a slow-motion take of two players walking off the field and the coach's telling one, "Stan, you have to feel the pressure closing in on you. Get focused or get the fuck off my team." In a rage, the coach flips the bench with water. Then there's a cut to a handheld shot and a shadow approaching the coach. The coach turns to the unseen figure: "Yeah? What?" Then we hear an extradiegetic, ominous, swift hissing sound. Fade to black and then to an interior shot at night of a meeting between a principal and teachers. The camera pans 360 degrees, introducing the teachers as the principal tells them: "Mrs. Brummel, sadly there's no computers . . . Mr. Tate, you're dreaming, absolutely no field trip to New York City . . . Mrs. Olson, there's just no money for a musical this year." As the pan comes to a stop and frames the principal, audiences would likely recognize her as Bebe Neuwirth playing the rigid character Dr. Lilith Sternin in the TV show *Frasier*. The principal tells the faculty that history and the arts don't matter and that football is all that matters.

With an economy of means (within two minutes of the film's opening) we already know that this will be a film about the tensions between hierarchies of authority: between the teenagers (high school) and adults (the coach as representative of other "faculty") as well as tensions between the principal and the teachers. While a few ominous and eerie sound bites are heard, the audience is seemingly within a conventional story set in a high school microcosm of hierarchies of interrelations. However, this soon changes. Four minutes into the film, Marco Beltrami's sound design (Beltrami scored *Scream* and *Mimic*) introduces a dramatically rising orchestrated off-chord score and screams meant to intensify our sense of horror. First stabbed by the coach, the principal runs, trapped inside a locked high school building. She's violently stabbed to death by the earlier meek-and-mild-appearing Mrs. Olson, now turned psychopathic killer: "I always wanted to do that."

The Faculty (1998). Comic-book introduction of Clea DuVall as the
loner goth character, Stokely "Stokes" Mitchell.

All this takes place before the film's title credit appears and the principal
teen characters are introduced. The mystery (the shadow seen on the football
field), horror (murderous psychopaths), and setting (high school) are established, but the audience is still not sure how these seemingly disparate ingredients will all come together. The audience knows this will be a teen-horror story
gravitating around hierarchies of power, but not exactly which of the slasher/
mystery or otherwise generic conventions will become dominant. This will only
become clear in the audience's mind twenty-six minutes into the film when
Mrs. Jessica Brummel (Susan Willis) enters the gym shower and the film audience sees through the point of view of high school jock Stan Rosado her monstrous, alien-like feet and then her pustulated face and body. The visuals along
with the disharmonious orchestra score firmly solidify the film within the conventions of horror.

Rodriguez shifts to a straightforward realist technique to shoot the exterior
of Herrington High School. Here Rodriguez shows a number of students arriv-
ing and milling around before the start of class for the day. The audience hears
the instrumental riff (Class of '99) of Pink Floyd's "Another Brick in the Wall"
overlay (in the extradiegetic channel) all the activity followed by the sound of
students talking. The sound of a muffler and then the sight of a black-and-red-
striped fish-tailing Camaro with tires screeching shift to another extradiegetic
sound: D Generation's "Helpless" (about standing in the shadows feeling alone
and how teachers "gave us bad religion/Stomach aches and scars"). Then the
music score shifts back to the Floyd riff the moment we see a blue and maroon
car collide; one blonde older girl pulls the other from her car and they start
fighting—all while scenes of other students colliding into each other walking

to class are intercut. Then Rodriguez's camera follows, then pauses as it introduces, each of the principal teen characters in a horror comic-book style: a splash of red writing superimposed over the film: Casey, Stokely, Delilah, Stan, Marybeth. He sets up yet another contract: this horror teen flick will at once be realist *and* comic book–like in its sensibility.

In his translation from words on a page (script) to film, we see Rodriguez's mastery of knowing how his audience will gap fill. A clear sense of his audience (one who will get the conventions of the principal genres at work here and who will understand the music cues) allows for an economy of means to be used in orchestrating the audio and visual elements together in such a way as to guide the audience to gap fill all that is left out. With the instrumental riff of Floyd's "Another Brick" the audience will recall the song that focuses on the theme of resistance to school and teachers as agents of mind control, of adults as not understanding teenagers ("no dark sarcasm in the classroom") and as seeing teens as a faceless multitude ("another brick in the wall"), of schoolchildren on a conveyer belt falling into a huge meat grinder in the music video (for the post-MTV generation).

The choice of visuals included in the opening scenes not only introduces the protagonists, but, without big sweeping aerial shots of the town, for instance, already gives us the feeling of the small-town setting. As the film unfolds, Rodriguez only shows us a couple of houses and streets beyond the high school grounds, knowing that the audience will fill in the necessary gaps; in our minds, the few houses and streets become many houses and streets that make up Herrington; the few police and parents actually seen (Casey's) become the many parents and police that make up the town police. Most of the film, that is, takes place in a few spaces on the school grounds — and mostly interior spaces; of course, the interior spaces intensify our sense of the trapped feel of the characters — intensifying our sense of the horror.

That is, Rodriguez knows well that the art of film is the art of what is chosen to be shown and *not* to be shown, to be heard and *not* to be heard. He knows well the art of cinema is not one of imitation and a one-to-one correspondence between reality and what is represented on the screen, but an artful reorganization of the building blocks of reality in such a way as to guide the audience's gap-filling mechanisms — the audience's imagination and therefore also the audience's emotions and thoughts generally.

Rodriguez's re-creation of Williamson's script refuses to dumb down or caricature the representation of teenage life. As the film unfolds and the mishmash of characters are forced more and more to interact with one another, we discover that each of the characters is more complicated than first meets the eye; the seeming academic loser, rebel, drug pusher, senior-year-repeating Zeke (Josh Hartnett) turns out to be a genius chemist, the jock Stan Rosado (Shawn

Hatosy) wants to quit quarterbacking and focus on his academics, and the loner goth character, Stokely "Stokes" Mitchell (Clea DuVall), is a repository of literary and cultural history. The stereotypical teen types become more complex as they are put under pressure and stress to figure out what is happening—in the library Stokes considers with Casey a parallel with *Invasion of the Body Snatchers*—and how to overcome the takeover of the high school and town by parasitic aliens who are invading the human bodies.

Rodriguez shows us how each character's individual psychology evolves under stress, how the story becomes less about the threat of alien invasion and more about how the teens behave collectively. And, once they overcome the obstacle of the alien invasion, these otherwise stock characters (jock, rebel, nerd, princess, loner) discover the freedom to exist in more complete and complex ways with one another and in their world. Normal, everyday life resumes at the high school, but the main characters relate to one another and the world differently. Stokely no longer wears black and is seen deeply in love with Stan; Stan is no longer a quarterback, and Zeke is seen playing football (albeit, still smoking) looking at the alien-invaded but now returned to human English teacher, Miss Elizabeth Burke (Famke Janssen); she smiles back giddily from the bleachers. Casey is the hero and gets the cheerleader in the end.

Rodriguez delivers a film that is at once realist in the sense that he uses realist film techniques (180-degree rule and seamless cuts to create a conventional Hollywood narrative effect) as well as comic-book conventions. Not only is the film self-aware of its function within the horror film genre—Stokely says after they kill Mr. Furlong (Jon Stewart of *The Daily Show*), "Isn't this the point when somebody says 'Let's get the fuck out of here'"—but as it moves more toward the convention of the sci-fi alien flick, it participates more in the storytelling mode of the grotesque. Rodriguez shows us how the alien invades the human body, penetrating the skin of the young teens (beautiful) and then visibly squirming under the skin. Near the end (1 hour 25 minutes) Zeke decapitates the alien-invaded Miss Burke only to see her head walk squid-like with tentacles reaching out to find her body. (This is also a John Carpenter moment. Rodriguez clearly alludes to the scene in *The Thing* when a decapitated head sprouts arachnid-like legs and walks away.) This is a moment of the grotesque: the beautiful (Janssen) and the ugly (tentacle-walking head). Indeed, Torben Grodal considers how our evolved neurobiological capacities allow us to at once seek out and derive pleasure from comical, "pleasure-evoking" films as well as tragic and "disgust-evoking" films (91). We have evolved emotion motivators (fear, lust, love, sadness, aggression) crucial for actions necessary for our survival.

As Grodal discusses, there is something central to our need to see things through in our everyday activities; to our "setting goals and making plans" (93)

The Faculty (1998). The school's teen newcomer, Marybeth (Laura
Harris), before she turns into a monster.

and therefore to overcoming obstacles "negative emotions are integrated into
the positive goals in such a way that the negative events pose activating challenges" (93). We are rewarded (dopamine and oxytocin release) for succeeding
in overcoming and attaining goals. Grodal carries this into the film experience,
discussing how "part of the arousal caused by a disgusting monster may be transformed to positively valenced emotions if the viewers simulate protagonists that
have sufficient coping potentials" (94). In other words, the pleasure of watching Casey use the bleacher stand in the school gym to crush the mother alien
(who turns out to be the school's teen newcomer, Marybeth, played by Laura
Harris) is intensified because of how disgusting the alien looks. We can see how
a director like Rodriguez manipulates our emotion of disgust in ways that intensify our pleasure when Casey vanquishes the threatening alien monster.

Finally, Rodriguez masterfully weaves into a conventional high school
slasher/horror flick a story about characters that, under pressure to work collectively, realize their potential to be more than a type. To overcome the obstacle — imminent threat and total takeover of human race by aliens — they sacrifice several of the adults: at the end, a news reporter voice-over mentions how
"life has returned to normal at Herrington High after the mysterious disappear-
ance of several faculty one month ago." Social harmony is restored but with the
seeming sacrifice of the principal and several of the teachers.

In his The Mind and Its Stories Patrick Colm Hogan identifies several universal prototype narratives, including that of the sacrificial narrative. In the last instance, The Faculty follows this narrative structure. It begins with some commu-

The Faculty (*1998*). *Marybeth after she turns into a monster.*

nal sin: impoverished learning environments, mistrust by the parents of their children, adult and teen hierarchies of power that end up in total destruction. (Recall, too, Casey's mention of *Schindler's List* and the date on the chalkboard in Mr. Tate's history class: 1941. Genocide does not require an alien invasion.) As per the conventions of the sacrificial prototype narrative, such a ripped social tissue (and not the disobeying of a god in earlier iterations of this universal story) results in communal devastation; this can only be reversed through communal sacrifice. Once the sacrifice is accomplished, the suffering ends. This also implies a certain ethics in *The Faculty*: that conformity and the use of social position (parent or teacher or popular student) for exploitation and individual gain are to be avoided for the regeneration of a full and healthy society where, like Stan, Stokely, Zeke, Casey, and even Miss Burke, all can realize their dreams, creativity, and capacities in the world.

Familia Redefined, Chocolate Rivers, Rainbow Rocks, Dreamscapes, and S'mores

I HAVE DISCUSSED ALREADY RODRIGUEZ'S KNACK FOR making films that appeal to specific audiences. Some consider this a shortcoming; I consider it a strength. Whether it's our taste or not doesn't really matter. What matters is whether or not the film succeeds in holding together its parts with this ideal audience in mind. So one might not be too partial to teen sci-fi/horror films but still recognize that all the parts that make up a film like *The Faculty* cohere to create a specific aesthetic relationship with the audience; as a whole it has a purposefully directed unity of affect. We see this to great success with the first installment of the *Spy Kids* franchise. It is a film that aims to capture the perspective, imagination, and emotions (pleasures of play and anxieties of potential loss) of children, and it does so with great unity of affect.

It is sometimes worth being reminded that children have already begun building and refining a discerning taste for stories they like and those they don't. Part of this like and dislike comes more from *how* the stories are told than *what* the story is about. After all, as a species we have only developed a handful of prototype narratives (epic, comic, tragic, sacrificial, say); of course, we have combined and recombined to an infinite degree these prototypical story structures, but they are still recognizable as based on a few.

As I already discussed earlier in the book, it is how a director like Rodriguez uses the visual and audio devices of filmmaking that gives unique shape to the story. It is this unique shape that can turn a child on or off to a film story. For instance, my seven-year-old daughter, Corina, watches *Spy Kids* over and over again, not for the story—she knows this so well she can even recite lines verbatim—but because of the visual and auditory tricks Rodriguez uses to give it shape. These can be anything from the choice of the gadgets—Machete products, the designed and built jet packs, to makeup tables where the push of a sequence of cosmetic lids activates holographic screens. It can also be the choice of derring-do, spy-thriller-sounding music; baroque interiors; contrastive reds, greens, and blues; the rhythm of the cutting from dynamic action with meditative reflection. Corina goes back time and time again because Rodriguez uses these formal elements to give dynamic shape to a story that captures, intensifies, and enhances the creative, exploratory mind of the child. (This is also why children like to read or listen to their parents read the same story over and over again—not for a content they know all too well, but for the author's choice of words, commas, images, tempo, and point of view, among many other shaping elements available for use.) I should add that I've tried other spy-kid-oriented films with Corina such as Robert Vince's flat *Spymate* (2006), the smart-aleck and irreverent *Shrek* (2001), and the politically correct yet ultra-violent *Brave* (2012). Shapeless and removed from the child's worldview (the directors' having in the forefront of their mind the parent taking the child), she spits them back out.

INDUSTRY

While shooting "The Misbehavers" in 1994 (part of the anthology movie *Four Rooms*) Rodriguez was struck by an image: with its protagonists Juancho (Danny Verduzco) and Sarah (Lana McKissack) dressed rather formally, he had the idea of making a film that focused on two Latino kids as James Bond–like spies; this gave shape to another idea he'd had when he was eleven years old—to make a movie focused on Latino kids. This idea would finally realize itself in his writing of the script, producing (in-house with Elizabeth Avellán), shooting, supervising special effects, editing, and sound mixing of the $36 million film, *Spy Kids 1*. (This is still a modest budget and relative steal given that *Inspector Gadget* was made for $90 million and had 200 fewer F/X shots.) He brought on Guillermo Navarro as his DP. And while he composed some of the music (along with Marcel Rodriguez) he brought on Los Lobos to perform some of the music tracks as well as film music composers John Debney and Danny Elfman. The film would be distributed by the Weinstein brothers' Dimension Films and released March 30, 2001. (Bob Weinstein had given him the green light to make a kid's spy movie at the Venice Film Festival in 1997, on condition that he direct what was just around the corner, *The Faculty*.) It grossed over $168 million worldwide—and millions more in video and merchandise sales.

"The Misbehavers" (1994). The title page from Rodriguez's comic-book storyboard.

Dimension entered its first-ever marketing promotion with McDonald's. Hence, when Carmen rehydrates a hamburger and fries in the safe house, when it pops out of the rehydrater we see the McDonald's Golden Arches. Indeed, McDonald's did well, piggybacking on the film's success by advertising spy gadgets with its Happy Meals. Unlike some films (Schumacher's Batmans or Alex Proyas's *I, Robot*, for instance) where the product placement takes over the story, engineering plot turns for the sake of making a product visible, here they simply exist as part of the storyworld. They don't get in the way of the story.

The film experienced both a tremendous commercial and critical success. It was the top-grossing kids' film of 2001. The film was nominated for many awards, and Rodriguez received an American Latino Media Arts (ALMA) award for Outstanding Director in a Motion Picture. And the media pundits

*"The Misbehavers" (1994). Sarah (Lana McKissack) and Juancho
(Danny Verduzco) dressed up and alone in their hotel room.*

were pleasantly surprised that its content was devoid of monsters, blood, and
gore. Elvis Mitchell comments that Rodriguez uses his "sugar-buzz filmmaking
style [. . .] for the good of family-kind" (12). Moreover, Mitchell discusses how
Rodriguez's carefully created film captures well a kid's "Play-Doh Fun Factory"
sensibility. Others remarked on the significance of Rodriguez's creating of
heroic Latino protagonists. Roger Ebert, for instance, states, "With a movie so
enchanting and cheerful, I want to resist sociological observations, but it should
be noted that Rodriguez has made a mainstream family film in which most of
the heroic roles are assigned to Hispanic characters (at one point, the Banderas
character even jokes about all the Latinos on Floop's TV show)" (http://www
.rogerebert.com/reviews/spy-kids-2001).

In addition to the mainstream accolades, the *Spy Kids* franchise films have
received academic attention. For instance, Phillip Serrato considers how Juni's
overcoming of his boyhood fears and anxieties would appeal to boy audiences.
For Serrato, Juni offers the possibility of transcending the challenges of boyhood and making real "a fantasy of empowerment" (forthcoming).

In Rodriguez's film world, Latinos simply exist. Just as it is normal that the
eight-year-old Juni (Daryl Sabara) and twelve-year-old Carmen (Alexa Vega)
become spy kids, so too is it normal that they are Latino. In this world, it is normal that people speak Spanish, that kids named Reynaldo attend elementary
school, and that one has uncles named Felix that look like Cheech Marin or
Danny Trejo; Trejo plays Isadore "Izzy" Cortez, the brother of Gregorio and in-
ventor of Machete spy products. It is normal that in Latino families parents and
children can look phenotypically very different, so Rodriguez casts Banderas as
Gregorio and Carla Gugino as Ingrid.

The film certainly falls within the generic conventions of the spy adventure; there is a mission — and a world to save. Here, however, figures morph into colorful singing human/animation hybrid mutants known as Fooglies (played in reverse, they are actually extending pleas for help), and robots made of giant thumbs appear; there are spy gadgets, but they are designed to capture the imagination of children. And Rodriguez knows well that the young film-going audience will take delight in the kid-sized jet packs and jet planes, electro-shock chewing gum, and cosmetic tables that turn into holographic screens, but the story doesn't obsess over the gadgets. (Unlike, say, Jon Favreau's *Iron Man*, where the story, camera lens, music, and nearly every other ingredient in the film becomes focused on the Iron Man suit.) Moreover, the gadgets exist in ways that deepen the comic-book sensibility of the film.

Rodriguez creates a comic-book world — in the sense that, like in comics and cartoons (those of Tex Avery especially), we enter a world where children like Juni and Carmen can encounter the huge dangers, yet they are safe. Often the real world feels menacing to children; adults tend to forget that children can feel very strong fears and anxieties about themselves and the world they inhabit. Rodriguez understands this well, creating characters like Juni, whose stress results in more warts; he attempts to conceal the warts with colorful Band-Aids. We see him express his anxiety about the warts in the bathroom — a space that Serrato identifies as "intrinsically associated — especially in childhood — with shame and the abject" (forthcoming). And, as Serrato further comments, it is this anxiety about not fitting in and being ugly that makes a show like *Floop's Fooglies* so attractive to Juni. It's filled with colorful and grotesque Fooglies led by Floop, who sings at one point: "If you follow me you can all be free! *Free!*" Floop and his Fooglies become a source of validation for Juni.

He invents the older sister, Carmen, who appears to be strong, fearless, and confident. Unlike Juni, who is in many ways still learning to manipulate objects in the world with dexterity and know-how, she seems to know how objects (gadgets) and adults (good and bad) work. When Juni fumbles, she's quickly ready with the invectives: "meat head," "warthog," and "booger breath." While Rodriguez paints Carmen realistically as an impatient older sibling, we discover more complexity to her character. She is in fact the one who wets her bed at night — usually a result of being anxious and aware of tension between parents and other adults yet without the capacity to understand fully its causes and consequences. Rodriguez knows that children can live in a world of fear. So he makes a film where the protagonists are the children; the responsibility of parents is to protect children, but they often do this by hiding things — having secrets and a secret life — that only add to the fears and anxieties.

Aware of the fact that children can live in fear, Rodriguez invents a film where fearful things happen but gives the children powers that we find in comic books. Powers to act and to face this fearful world. Powers to overcome one's fears and to attain victory not only over their fears but also the cause of their fears. Juni and Carmen save the parents, and by saving them, they save the unity of the family, thus restoring the safe haven of the family structure and unit. Rodriguez ends *Spy Kids 1* with the family gathered together, including the erstwhile estranged brother, Isadore "Izzy" (of Machete spy gadgets) in front of the computer monitor talking to leader of the OSS (Organization of Super Spies), Devlin (George Clooney). The reassertion of family at the end of film is also reassuring for children.

Children filmgoers can also experience the dangers and anxieties that fill up the world, and they do so immersed in the secure, comforting space of the fiction of the film. They return again and again to the film because it reassures them that it will all be fine in the end. While children are not aware of this directly, they intuit a world that appears to be pulling apart at the seams. In today's society, more and more, the family unit is turned into its opposite—a repressive institution. You find all kinds of aberrations in family: incest, domestic violence, sexual exploitation, etc. Since this is the society we live in, and this society has not yet created any kind of valid substitute for the family unit as an institution, the destruction of family weakens each member of the unit. Rodriguez's film locates in the family this explicit will to preserve it as a whole unit. He knows this is reassuring for children, and as a collateral consequence, that it is also reassuring for the parents watching the film with their children.

The general device of the film is the cartoon, and its aesthetic is to a large degree the grotesque such as the Fooglies and Thumb Thumbs (inspired by creatures he imagined and drew as an eleven-year-old), the villain Floop's robot kids, and the baroque interiors and exterior such as the Cortez's house and Floop's castle.

All these creatures, structures, and images are made up of the aesthetic of the grotesque. Here it is made to serve the purposes of telling a story that, like comic books, is reassuring for children. Rodriguez purposefully created a comic-book film—in sensibility only and not in execution. He wanted to use real actors playing characters experiencing real, everyday dilemmas; as such, the child filmgoers can enjoy and laugh as they vicariously experience the overcoming of dangerous situations.

This elaborate film—its rich palette of colors, baroque architecture, and interior designs, its agents-cum-Fooglie monsters, and the transformation of the beautiful in the case of the spy Ms. Gradenko (Teri Hatcher), whose hair catches on fire, becoming the embodiment of the beautiful and ugly—adds up to a whole aesthetic experience of the grotesque. From the beginning to the end

Spy Kids (2000). Floop's baroque castle.

of the film, the grotesque strictly serves the essential goal of reassuring children, like comic books and cartoons, that in spite of their fears, anxieties, and nightmares, all will be ok. (Rodriguez uses the same hair-burning event in *Roadracers*. Just after Teddy's girlfriend hurls racist epithets at the Latina character Donna, her hair catches alight; in the aftermath, she appears scary, ugly, and witch-like; her exterior mirrors an interior filled to the brim with ugly, gnarled prejudice.) Rodriguez's expertise and strong awareness of what it means to be a child (pleasures and fears) allow him to create *Spy Kids 1* according to the principles of the comic-book/cartoon sensibility because of his use precisely of the aesthetic means and goals of the grotesque. At one point, Carmen tells Juni: "Never send adults to do a kid's job." We might qualify this here, adding, "unless you have the imagination and ingenuity of a kid" as Rodriguez does.

SPY KIDS 2: THE ISLAND OF LOST DREAMS (2002)

*F*OLLOWING ON THE HEELS OF *SPY KIDS 1* DIMENSION Films released, to great commercial success, its sequel on August 7, 2002. Made for $38 million, *Spy Kids 2* brought in nearly $120 million in worldwide ticket sales.

This was yet another moment of feverish productivity for Rodriguez. He overlapped the making of *Spy Kids 2* with the scripting (in two weeks) and shooting (in seven weeks) of *Once Upon a Time in Mexico*. Even though Harvey Weinstein offered him more money ($60 million) to film the sequel—allowing him to hire more crew, possibly, to ease any burdens of production, he chose to serve as director, writer, editor, coproducer, production designer, songwriter, and music composer (with John Debney). To keep the costs down, too, Rodriguez filmed in and around Austin, San Antonio, and Arlington, only taking Daryl Sabara and Alexa Vega abroad to film the Costa Rica shots. He recycled from the first installment where possible, as with the big-budget push-in shot to the Cortez residence at the edge of the sea that opens the film.

With his hand in all aspects of the making of the film, Rodriguez knew exactly where to spend time and money. For instance, he could determine exactly what needed to be built to create a sense of a set filled with boulders; knowing that a sequence will only have three shots, rather than build an entire set with twenty-five boulders, they could build one with only three boulders that they could move around on wheels to fill out the background of each of the three shots; a scene when Juni and Carmen enter a Mayan-like temple only needs a set of stairs. (See the "Ten Minute Film School" included on the DVD.) Although Rodriguez spent $38 million to make the sequel, given the use of new HD and green screen technology, and that most sequels cost on average double that of the original, this was filmmaking still at its most magical and efficient.

Rodriguez can save time and money because he uses his filmmaking skills along with his acute sense of how a given audience will imagine details that are not shown. He has a very astute and rich sense of how audiences fill in the gaps—he knows how our visual and auditory perceptual systems will be triggered and in which direction—therefore using CGI and animation special effects (with lead animator Gregor Punchatz), along with his HD camera and green screen technology, to great visual effect. (He used twice as many special effects here as in the first installment.) Knowing what to actually build and what to fill in with CGI also proves significant; Rodriguez knows well that the perceptual system needs a reality anchor in order for the mind/brain to make the rest (the CGI) feel as if real. He knows, too, how to vary the visual rhythm of the special effects. For instance, he chooses to give a stop-motion effect to the sequence when Juni and Carmen fight marauding skeletons. This not only alludes to an earlier era of imaginative filmmaking that the parent filmgoers would likely pick up on and enjoy, recalling childhood memories of Ray Harryhausen's creations for *Jason and the Argonauts*, for instance, but it offers a perceptual shift in how the audience engages with the action. This and other special effects and animation choices convey a comic-book vibrancy rather than seamless realism. Rodriguez knows just how the audience will perceive and then interpret the shots as they make up sequences of meaning—and all this to the millisecond.

The film opens and firmly establishes this comic-book contract with the viewer. Rodriguez sets his audience in Troublemaker amusement park with the owner Dinky Winks (Bill Paxton) introducing to Alexandra such rides as the Vomiter and the Juggler. Alexandra is there with bodyguards, but not her father. He's too busy to spend time with her—a common thread throughout all of Rodriguez's child-oriented films, where we see this focus on children's fear of abandonment and anxiety about not being important enough for a parent to spend time with them. Her plan to sabotage the Juggler to get her father to pay her attention and spend time with her doesn't go as planned, so Juni and Carmen are brought in for the rescue—along with the brother–sister spy-kid team and rivals, Gary (Matt O'Leary) and Gerti Giggles (Emily Osment). This launches the plot that involves the two spy-kids teams using their smarts and physical dexterity to retrieve the Transmooker device (a device that can disable the world's electricity) from a mysterious island, home to the scientist Romero (Steve Buscemi). On the island, the two brother–sister teams are archrivals—even dueling to seeming death with Romero's hybrid monsters. However, in the end the two brother–sister teams become friends.

Once again, Rodriguez is tuned to the kinds of everyday actions and emotions of children, building a story that allows for the vicarious experience of this within the safe zone of fictional play. This is what happens in real life with children and is something they dislike about reality: they enter into conflict with their peers. Phillip Serrato locks onto the dynamic established between Gary and Juni, remarking how "Gary functions as an ego ideal incarnate, and as such he carries the potential to induce anew inferiority and humiliation in Juni. Gary is tall, blond, slim, and overall well-groomed and good-looking, which stands in contrast to Juni's stout build" (forthcoming). As Serrato explains, Juni's anxiety at being displaced by Gary comes to a head when he sees a janitor replace his Spy Kid of the Year photo with one of Gary. However, Juni's journey includes growing the psychological strength to see Gary for what he is: a bad kid. In fact it is Juni and not the worldly wiser Carmen who recognizes this. Juni tells her, "You like him and believe him? Gary's a bad guy, Carmen." As Juni finds strength of character and Gary a sense of humiliation, there's reconciliation. The film ends happily when Juni and Carmen become friends with Gary and Gerti—a typical pattern of interaction seen with kids and their friends. Ultimately, the film makes safe those commonplace conflicts and anxieties experienced by children.

I should mention that, while the story focuses on the children (their action and emotions), Rodriguez includes a nod toward an adult emotion system that experiences crystallized reminders of a sense of becoming redundant in the rapidly developing life of a child. When Gregorio (Banderas) combs Juni's hair back (a deliberate allusion to and pull from the parallel scene in "The Misbehavers"), he tells him that "this is important and that once combed, you'll look cool. . . . In fact, you're looking cool already like me, like *papi*" and that it is "kind of emotional to me." Following this exchange Gregorio gestures toward helping Juni with his tie, but Juni commands his bug-robot "Ralph" to do the job. While this isn't Juni doing the work, it is his agency that directs the action of the tying of the bow; it is a sequence Rodriguez includes for the adults in the audience. Whether a parent or not, we understand and even feel empathy for Gregorio, whose perplexed, hurt look expresses this sense of no longer being needed by the child. He insists: "Interesting, but he can never replace me."

MAMBO AND MORE

The hair-combing/bow-tying scene between Gregorio and Juni points to another element included in the film—that of a Latinidad that simply exists, and playfully so. At the OSS ball, Gregorio has a Latino machismo moment, interrogating Gary about what kinds of dances he knows: Tango? Mambo? Rumba? Cha-cha-cha? Bossa nova? Merengue? or Waltz? Once he proves himself the macho *papí*, he struts off stage left. Of course, the scene is choreographed in such a way that it comes off with great playfulness, self-mockingly playing up the Latino macho role. As with other of Rodriguez's films, Latinidad simply is a perfectly integrated and natural part of the characterizations. Gregorio simply is a special agent (named after Rodriguez's uncle who is an FBI special agent); Cheech Marin simply is "uncle" Felix; every time Juni and Carmen call him uncle, he reminds them he's not their uncle, playfully calling attention to that tradition in Latino families of calling any close family friend "uncle." Danny Trejo simply is Uncle Isador, or Izzy "Machete" Cortez; he's that uncle who builds things for the kids, but in this case a high-tech tree house and holographic wristwatches that do everything except tell time. It's a world where Latinos simply exist, including as Troublemaker amusement park public relations officer played by Rodriguez's sister, Angela Lanza. It's a world where mysterious islands don't have an Anglo Dr. Moreau, but rather a scientist named Romero—and an Aztec–Mayan temple to boot. It's a world where Latino grandparents appear as dark or light skinned, English is spoken with a thick Spanish accent, or no trace of one. It's a world that makes natural the presence of Latinos in all their variety.

Above all, Rodriguez seeks to create a storyworld aimed to satisfy and extend the imagination of children. He does this by infusing this world with a comic-book or cartoon sensibility, using the visuals and auditory channels of the film to do so. He intensifies the sound of the WHOOSH of Juni's sword and the POW of the brawling centaur–spider against the snake–lizard, or slizzard, for instance. All this works to give it that comic-book or cartoon feel that is so appealing to children. It is within this space, as I mentioned already, that children can experience the kind of antagonisms with their social peers as well as anxieties about adults that are ultimately resolved in a way that soothes. And technically, Rodriguez makes the experience of this feel new and vital.

There is much in the film that slips into an adult, non-comic-book, say, mind-set. There is the introduction of emotions and desires that are above, say, the pay grade of Juni and Carmen—flirting, love interests, and moral dilemmas—much of which might not appeal to the age range of children the film targets. For instance, there is the moral dimension of the story that appeals to an older audience. Gerti has to choose between family (evil-doing father who has been doing bad things to people for years to infiltrate the oss and become director) and saving humanity. This is a rather large burden. Carmen tells Gerti that she will know at the right time what is right.

This right and wrong choice is a moral decision. Yet, children are not socialized enough to really care about moral options and decisions. They are essentially amoral; little by little they acquire a sense of right and wrong, but this is a process that takes time. We're not born with this compass—rules of interaction with other humans in society. There are a whole series of behavioral traits that are more akin to the adult than to the child, even though they are still children, but older children. This is to say, whereas in the first installment we had clear-cut good and bad guys and their actions that captured well the spontaneity and naïveté of children and that led to great aesthetic satisfaction and catharsis of the child, here it is lacking. When Romero explains to Carmen and Juni that their falling toward the center of the earth was an illusion, we might ask this question: why explain this at all when kids want to experience this in a cartoon-like way, and not have it explained? And during the ball when Juni demonstrates his prowess as a ballet dancer, the audience is expected to understand the incongruity between the child and what he's doing; this triggers our laughter—the laughter of adults because children will not care about this incongruity.

Rodriguez brings to the fore this sense of a child's life as full of confusions and insecurities—many of which grow from the contradictory behavior of adults. Kids need to be reassured that they are loved and protected. Just as in *Spy Kids 1*, in this installment we see the kids as the heroes, doing all the heavy lifting as they overcome dangers and at the same time that they want all kinds of protections and reassurances. Comic books and cartoons are very cathartic in this sense; the bad guy can be beaten up and reduced to pulp by whatever form of punishment; misunderstood bad guys can also become good guys as with Floop. Here there's no physical or social punishment and there's no repentance. In a world that is already very confusing for children, shades of gray are less satisfying; they feel satisfied by the black and white in behavior and punishment.

In *Spy Kids 1* Rodriguez is very perceptive and sensitive to the psychological insecurities and fears of small children. He created a narrative fiction that allowed young filmgoers to experience such fears and anxieties within the comfort zone of a film with a comic-book sensibility. He provided a protective space whereby the child filmgoer could vicariously work through such negative emotions. Acutely aware of how children fill in gaps in stories, Rodriguez chose carefully what to show and what not to show, offering the young audience the opportunity to imagine even more expansively gadgets, creatures, and structures. As with any sequel, the challenge is how to keep this up. The challenge is how to *make new* when the character origins and overall plotlines have been established. With *Spy Kids 2* Rodriguez chooses to introduce the preoccupations and worldview of children (Juni) *and* pre-adolescents (Carmen).

In many ways this is a smart move and anticipates the fast-growing biological development of his child actors Daryl Sabara and Alexa Vega. However, in so doing, the film might be more likely to fall between the cracks of two audiences, so to speak. It's a film that doesn't exactly address teenagers (the protagonists are not yet teens), and yet much of its content seems aimed at teens. I think of the OSS ball when Juni courts the president's daughter, Alexandra (Taylor Momsen). While the tango-dance scene charmingly parodies the Latino macho ways, I wonder if Juni's interest in Alexandra appears to represent more the emotion-set of a teenager or an adult than young boy. Of course, the incongruity of the scene—Juni's age and his action—is what makes us as adults laugh, but it's we adults laughing. Carmen is not quite a teen yet exhibits teenager traits. For instance, she forgives Gary Giggles (Matt O'Leary) for being a bad boy; for doing things that are morally reprehensible. She's willing to overlook this because she's attracted to him, stating even at one point, "I think I can change him." It's not that there is anything wrong with this, of course. It's that perhaps here, unlike *Spy Kids 1*, Rodriguez advances too quickly the actions of the characters to behavior and emotions more akin to the teen set—something that would be difficult at best for a young five- to eleven-year-old audience to gap fill and imagine and make the story theirs.

While Rodriguez is technically masterful at guiding how his audience gap fills the "natural environment," the biological and social gaps in *Spy Kids 2* become harder to negotiate for young audiences; many of the gaps can't be filled in simply because of the biology of any given child filmgoer that has yet to develop his or her biological mappings in terms of sexual desire and interest, as well as in terms of cultural mappings in the sense of the age-dependent understanding of what it means for a parent (Gregorio in this case) to not receive the anticipated career promotion.

One might argue that while commercially successful with real audiences, in terms of its content and form coming together to cohere as an organic whole, because of this mixing of child with teen psychological levels *Spy Kids 2* is arguably not as unified and straightforward as the first film in terms of who the ideal audience would be and therefore what kind of gap filling has to be done. As I already suggested, this might be a difficulty posed by the age of the actors: Sabara is still a young boy and Vega is a preteen, thus making the characters they play ambiguous, liminal, or in-between. However, the story appears much in advance of the age of both characters, asking the audience to be guided by characters who appear to be one age yet act another age. This is certainly an incongruity the audience (the children and parents) senses. Perhaps this is why, as writer for *Sight & Sound* Vicky Wilson remarks, her seven-year-old daughter, who, in comparing it with the first installment, missed "the humour of the extended gadget gags, [...] the slapstick generated by the bumbling robot thumbs (the first film's undoubted scene-stealers), and the constant bickering between Carmen and Juni that rendered their relationship so realistic" (52). Her daughter's concluding assessment: "Carmen's love interest and the tensions between Gregorio and his in-laws were a poor substitute" (53).

SPY KIDS 3-D: GAME OVER (2003)

WORKING AT HIS TRADEMARK PRODIGIOUS AND relentless pace, Rodriguez had ready to exhibit his third installment in the *Spy Kids* story by the summer of 2003. (Recall that he also had ready *Once Upon a Time in Mexico* for release that autumn.) Dimension Films released *Spy Kids 3-D* on July 25, 2003. It opened at number one at the box office, foretelling of what would become a tremendous commercial success. It would go on to bring in $200 million worldwide.

Having mastered the use of HD and green screen filmmaking with *Spy Kids 2* and *Once Upon a Time in Mexico*, Rodriguez decided this third installment would be an opportunity to resuscitate yesteryear's 3-D experience of, say, André de Toth's *House of Wax* (1953) but with twenty-first-century technology. He had been attracted to the idea since being introduced to the new 3-D technology with James Cameron's *Titanic* documentary *Ghosts of the Abyss*. He wanted the third installment to be the first feature-length film to use this technology—and for a budget of $39 million.

To pull off the huge amount of special effects (700 stereoscopic digital effects alone) required months of research and design. Rodriguez wanted the film to visually re-create a video game world—but with a lurid and slightly imperfect texture. He wanted to be sure, too, that all this could be exhibited on regular exhibition projectors, and not the IMAX 3D screens exclusive to but a few theaters nationally. By placing his 24P HD cameras side by side like eyes, he could aim at a convergence point and shoot as if looking from a left- and right-eye position simultaneously. (For more on this see Doyle.) A monitor with red/cyan anaglyph filtration glasses allowed him to see instantly whether he was successful at creating the stereoscopic effect. The digital technology allowed Rodriguez and his digital effects supervisor Chris Olivia (Troublemaker digital studio) to send files to other special effects teams such as, for instance, Janimation (who created effects for Level 1), Hybride Technologies (Level 2), Computer Café (Level 4), and The Orphanage (Level 5). Indeed, as the final credits attest, the long list of people involved in the visual effects count in the hundreds.

Nine minutes into the film we see why this installment required such a huge force of CGI and other visual effects talent. Soon after we hear Juni musing Mickey Spillane–style (and a visual–verbal pun on "gumshoe") about life as a freelance private investigator who has broken from the OSS — a very young Selena Gomez has a cameo as one of his clients, Waterpark Girl — he's brought back on board with the OSS and whisked into the video game world of Game Over to save his sister Carmen. The film takes place mostly in the video game environment — all of which is in 3-D. Indeed, most of the film (sixty-six minutes out of the total eighty minutes) is in 3-D.

Juni must reach Level 4 of Game Over to save Carmen (a hacker specialist as it turns out) and then Level 5 to destroy the game — a game invented by the Toymaker (Sylvester Stallone) to enslave all of the world's youth so he can take over the world. It's *The Faculty*, but wearing a video-game guise. With only twelve hours to complete his mission — once the cyberspace video game goes live, kids will plug in and then become trapped inside — Juni must overcome challenges presented by each level, including competing with various avatars: beta-testers, Francis (Bobby Edner), Arnold (Ryan Pinkston), Rez (Robert Vito), and Demetra (Courtney Jines). Along the way, he develops a crush of sorts on Demetra and enlists the help of his Grandfather Valentin Avellán (Ricardo Montalbán).

Juni must learn how to play the game in order to move up the levels. As Serrato comments, "Juni must navigate the unfamiliar landscape of the game and learn the rules that govern this realm reflect the ways that adolescence can be a baffling and frustrating time in life when one struggles to figure out and accommodate oneself to the adult world" (forthcoming). As he moves up the levels, his antagonists become accomplices so he can reach Level 5, where they encounter a knight in shining (video game) armor, "The Guy" (Elijah Wood), who opens the door. While they manage to destroy Game Over, Toymaker and his gorilla-like giant robots escape from cyberspace into reality, causing havoc and destruction. To vanquish Toymaker, Juni and Carmen enlist the help of their parents, uncles, and even members of their "extended" family such as Romero, Fegan Floop, Minion, and Dinky Winks (and his son), as well as friends Gary and Gerti Giggles.

As with the other *Spy Kids* installments, the final unity of family (and here extended family) is of central importance — and this for all the reasons given above. It is within the family that children first learn how to direct their emotions into activities identified as right and wrong. And Juni's journey in this film is about his facing challenges that test his sense of right and wrong — with the ultimate reward of the unity of *familia* — Latino and otherwise. However, and to no fault of the ever exploratory Rodriguez, the video game conceit might allow for only the display of the emotion of competition; video games based on such a simple and singular emotion (*Halo* and *Metroid* are mentioned in the film) might not be a capacious enough envelope to allow for an adequate portrayal of Juni's coming into a sense of how emotions link to actions that link to questions of wrong and right doing.

VIRTUAL WORLDS

This is not so much about audience — six- to twelve-year-olds certainly play video games. It is more about the use of the video game as a conceit or formal structure for the story. It has proven difficult for filmmakers (Steven Lisberger's 1982 *Tron* and Joseph Kosinski's 2010 follow-up, *Tron: Legacy*, for instance) to translate or re-create the video game environment in film, not because of technological constraints, but because of the qualitative difference between our experience of both: film is a very passive fictional format; we are certainly moved emotionally, but this happens while we sit and view the film; the emotions we experience when playing video games are triggered *in the playing* of the video games. If a video game such as Game Over existed as a real video game to play, it would be designed for the movement of buttons or toggles for repeated encounters with danger, triggering constantly the appraisal mechanism as expressed in further actions (what we would do next) to win *and not lose*. In fact, it is the player's action-oriented dexterity that intensifies the immersion and therefore also the emotive payoff. Because video games work primarily in this manner, films that use the win/lose video game aesthetic and the video game goals will only allow for a limited number of emotions to be experienced by the character and therefore the audience. Film requires thicker plots and characterizations.

Importantly, too, while the aesthetic of the games can be very baroque and filled with the simultaneous ugly and beautiful, they don't work in the same mode as the comic-book grotesque aesthetic. Unlike the comic-book grotesque aesthetic where we see and experience the dangers of defying all sorts of natural and social laws, but always end up whole in the end, the dangers in video games are not dangers at all; we don't perceive them as such when playing the video game because it is not based on any kind of assumption that there are dangers. The dangers are just obstacles to be surmounted in order to win the game. Moreover, the video game aesthetic is in many ways opposite to the comic-book grotesque, whose central ingredient is the irreverent, rebellious, and the carnivalesque. The video game adheres strictly to rules; every single ingredient in the video game is an algorithm based on digital binary 1/1 or 0/1. You can't play a video game without obeying to the dot absolutely and blindly the rules of the game; the moment I begin to play, I am trapped by the rules. The moment I accept to play the game, I accept to be a blindly strict rule follower.

This is a lengthy way of stating that the use of the video game format is not capacious enough for the range of emotions and action and thoughts of a character like Juni; it constrains the behavior between him and the other characters and the range of emotions and moral choices that might ensue. It restricts the aesthetic creativity and aesthetic enjoyment of the film.

Rodriguez's exploratory move to bring back to life the use of 3-D technology in the making and experiencing of film is laudable. He was the first to do so with feature filmmaking in the service of narrative fiction film storytelling. This would be a technique that he sharpens and that he absolutely integrates into the story in *Spy Kids 4D*, but here it functions as a kind of training ground, testing the capacities and limits of 3-D filmmaking all while honing skill with this new technology. I think Kimberley Jones of the *Austin Chronicle* sums it up best: "Rodriguez concentrates so heavily on the special effects that everything else — dialogue, acting, character and story development — comes off like an afterthought."

SPY KIDS 4D: ALL THE TIME IN THE WORLD (2011)

ONE COULD ARGUE THAT WITHOUT THE TRAINING experienced with 3-D in the making of *Spy Kids 3-D* we would not have the successful integration of this storytelling technology and means into the aesthetic that makes up *Spy Kids 4D: All the Time in the World*. The 3-D effects do not call attention to themselves. Rather, they give a sense of depth to the storyworld, allowing the audience to perceive simultaneously a sharp sense of foreground and background. The 3-D effects are used to give an added visual thickness to the film. Rodriguez fully integrates the 3-D effects into the experience of the movie as a unified whole.

What began as an idea on the set of *Machete* (2010) — Jessica Alba's then one-year-old's diaper exploding with poop — became the seed that would grow into the story for this fourth installment of the *Spy Kids* story. Rodriguez took the idea of a spy mom, wrote a script, and with a budget of $27 million, he began filming on October 27, 2010. Working along with some of his creative and technical stalwarts such as music designer Carl Thiel (on *Sin City, Machete, Planet Terror*), editor Dan Zimmerman (Rodriguez's produced *Predators*), and Austin-based DP Jimmy Lindsey (many Rodriguez films), less than a year after production began, Dimension Films released *Spy Kids 4D*. It opened on August 19, 2011, and brought in $11.6 million that weekend. While its opening didn't receive the same feeding frenzy at the box office as the earlier *Spy Kids* films, it would bring in a healthy $123 million worldwide.

Ever seeking ways to enrich the cinematic experience, Rodriguez adds to the textured perceptual experience (3-D) the sensation of smell. This, of course, had been tried before in the late 1950s and early 1960s when Walter Reade Jr. released Carlo Lizzani's travelogue *Behind the Great Wall* in what was called AromaRama and soon after when Hans Laube employed his Smell-O-Vision system whereby thirty different odors would spray during the showing of *Scent of Mystery*. These attempts were short-lived, and for biological reasons most likely. Just as it is difficult to give our sense of taste a discernible shape, so too is it difficult to give smell an identifiable shape. While the olfactory sense can be given shape — educated and trained into individual separate wholes — this is done by only a few specialists working in perfume and other businesses. For the great majority of us, we have a very limited range of reactions to smells. We make sense of them as simply either nice or repulsive. That's it. To make smells *make sense* in the experience of a film that privileges sight and sound is very difficult at best. If present, it likely serves either as an appendage that distracts or no contribution to the aesthetic means that will further the aesthetic goals in the film; it distracts because it leads the viewer to believe that the smell *will* be a part of the global aesthetic of film, but because it can't contribute in such a way, it creates a frustration on the part of the viewer.

While Rodriguez includes the sense dimension of smell — at the theaters rather ineffective scratch cards (all the smells were alike) were handed out with the 3-D glasses — the fourth dimension didn't modify the story whatsoever; it was subordinate to an already integrated use of the 3-D technology with the story. You could pick up and scratch the card or not, and the experience of the film would not be any more *or* less.

From the poopy diaper idea, Rodriguez creates a story that follows the adventures of Marissa Wilson, who is a mom to a newborn, Maria, and to her two stepchildren, Cecil and Rebecca Wilson. As the story unfolds, we discover that she's Gregorio and Machete Cortez's sister—Juni and Carmen's aunt. The film establishes immediately that she's also a spy, who must capture Tick Tock (Jeremy Piven) and then the Timekeeper (Jeremy Piven)—the archvillain who threatens to stop time and destroy the world.

I have mentioned before Rodriguez's knack for casting—not only in casting well-known actors in films that might appear to be déclassé, but also in his choice of actors. To play the role of the spy mama, Marissa, he casts Jessica Alba. While some critics missed the presence of Carla Gugino, Alba's eyes and expression bring a young, fresh vitality as well as believability to the double role: mama and superhero. Rodriguez establishes her character from the very beginning of the film. She is roundly pregnant yet still able to apprehend the bad guy; she does as she would sans baby—like sliding over the hood of a car as would be seen in any respectable action film, but of course slowly and holding her tummy. She naturalizes the fact that Latinas can also be spy mom superheroes, and she also makes quite natural the awkward experience many have with being a stepmom. Importantly, too, Rodriguez made the choice to cast unknowns for the parts of the children: Rowan Blanchard as Rebecca and Mason Cook as Cecil. The audience doesn't bring adjectival baggage to characters played by unknowns; casting well-known actors can make it more of a challenge for a director to have audiences think of the characters in ways independent of their prior roles. They play ordinary kids to an ordinary father, Wilbur Wilson, played

Spy Kids 4D (2011). Jessica Alba as the pregnant spy Marissa about to apprehend Tick Tock.

Spy Kids 4D (*2011*). *The dog Argonaut (voiced by Ricky Gervais) uses his in-built robotic gadget to transport the baby Maria.*

by a non-A-list actor—the relative newcomer to feature films Joel McHale. He can play the role of the ordinary father who discovers that he's more resourceful than he expected, inventing the Spy Finder gadget and ready to spring into action and perform the extraordinary when necessary. Even the choice to have the dog character Argonaut (voiced by Ricky Gervais) played by an unexceptional looking mutt (in actual fact a dog that was rescued from a local shelter) also emphasizes this sense of the ordinary becoming extraordinary in the story; we discover that Argonaut is anything but ordinary.

By choosing good, solid actors that are not universally known faces, Rodriguez leaves open all the expectancies of the characters; he gives the actors a lot of freedom to play their roles. The casting choice, then, makes all the more dramatic the character traits that are revealed as the story unfolds. The ordinary members of the family discover their own exceptional capacities, performing heroic deeds that don't depend on, say, their good looks or cutes. At the end, even the ordinary baby Maria ends up taking a first step, and then, in a Tex Avery moment, tosses a bad guy over her head. All the actors are at the service of the story, including the dog Argo. And, while we know front and center that Marissa is extraordinary—this is the antagonism that gives energy to the film— at the same time, she shows extraordinary behavior in very ordinary behavior: she loves the kids even though biologically they are not her kids.

The realizing of the film's aesthetic aims—from the writing through casting, shooting, editing, and scoring—matches well the perceptions, thoughts, and feelings of its intended audience: those children between six and twelve years old portrayed approximately by Cecil and Rebecca. This is confirmed by the less than objective audience response at my house with my seven-year-old and her six- and seven- and nine- and twelve-year-old cousins—the older ones simply like it, but wouldn't watch it again and again and again as Corina and her younger cousins do. They notice and enjoy the reversal of gender norms—Rebecca sits in a blue chair rocket and Cecil in a pink one; they experience tremendous pleasure at the sight of Juni and Carmen as adults; Cecil and Rebecca's introduction to the earlier Spy Kids gadgets is thrilling; they relish the new gadgets like the Hammer Hands and regular everyday objects retooled for spy work like Cecil's turning up the volume on his hearing aid to uncover Danger D'Amo's (Jeremy Piven) true identity as the Timekeeper; they discover that the villain is multiplied many times over under masks that look like clocks; they are surprised to discover that the head of the good guys D'Amo as director of oss is actually the head of the bad guys. Mostly, they are surprised at why the good guy and bad guy are one. It is not out of greed for power or any other pseudo-psychological explanation. It's that he wants to go back in time to be with his father, who was too busy with his lab experiments to spend time with him. In fact, Rodriguez takes this theme a step further in the story. D'Amo, as it turns out, is accidentally frozen in time in the father's lab, watching his father age and then die while he remains a child. His yearning to return to turn back the hands of time is a desire to relive his childhood with his father. However, by playing with time, he messes with the natural order of things, threatening to destroy the earth.

The older age range (nine- to twelve-year-old) children tend to notice more the stepmom issues as well as the way the film makes literal many of the metaphors about time. Aunties and uncles appreciate the skill in imagining the settings that are so surprising and how the film as a whole is clever and aesthetically appealing. They tend to comment more on how well the story is put together along with its visual experience and achievement. In a perfectly effortless way, they seem to enjoy watching the children view the film, imagining what it would be like to be a child having so much fun. In a word, they are the ideal audience.

Indeed, as the story unfolds we discover Rodriguez's use of the doppelgänger conceit once again. Here it is literalized. Tick Tock (Jeremy Piven) is a double, another iteration of the Timekeeper (Jeremy Piven) from a different time/place. Then we discover that the Timekeeper is actually the director of the oss, Danger D'Amo (Jeremy Piven); the letters unscrambled, Cecil discovers, spell Armageddon. ("I guess I'm not who you thought I was," Danger tells Marissa, Carmen, and Juni.)

Children relish the film's unraveling of the multiplying of identities. They also enjoy Rebecca's pranks, and Tick Tock's constant rhyming brings giggles. All the gags that belong to the aesthetic of the grotesque such as vomit, poop, and fart jokes trigger bellyaching laughs; they especially like it when Argonaut asks Cecil to pull his paw and he farts *for fart's sake*.

Adults and children alike, of course, experience the Tex Avery spirit of the film — not only the grotesque elements, but also the safety in which the children can face their anxieties and dangers vicariously through Cecil, Rebecca, and the baby Maria; they might get knocked around and fall, but then they get up whole. That is, the visuals, the aesthetic, and the story — the aesthetic aims and means — are in perfect consonance.

In the end, of course, this is a movie for children. It explores some of the anxieties of children today: more and more families are ad hoc, with new stepmoms, stepdads, and the like — and this is statistically less because of a death of a spouse, and more because of divorce and remarriage. For instance, the relationship between Cecil and Rebecca toward Marissa is one of antagonism built out of fear. Rebecca is cautious about the stepmom, not knowing if this new family member — new mom — feels affection for her. Cecil and Rebecca get to know something special about Marissa — she's a spy — and they also come to realize that she considers them special (her children) too.

The film also, of course, expresses different anxieties children have concerning time for children — both in the sense of growing up and also in the way adults take for granted the time in the presence of their children, and therefore do not consider time spent with them as special time. Cecil and Rebecca make it clear to the Timekeeper how pointless it is to try to turn the clock back, not so much in the making of a time machine, but commonsense experientially: "You can't change the past. There is no going back. The special moments are the ones we will remember. It is not how much time you have. It is what you choose to do with it." (Of course, adults in the audience will also be moved: if we have any regrets it's that of not taking full advantage of the time we can spend with our children.)

While Rodriguez returns to the theme of time as embodied in the dreamlike state of multiplying avatars of the same self, it springs from the central ideological generator of the story: the family. Undoubtedly this is *the* central, paramount concern of the child because family is the source of protection, security, affection, and sustenance. And, because of the careful internal logic of the story, it coheres well. Even extended family in the characters of Juni and Carmen are integrated in a well-established logical way. They are brought back into the story to protect (Carmen) and vanquish (Juni) the Tick Tock. The sibling rivalry continues to ripple under the surface. After having disappeared, Juni appears to steal the thunder from Carmen as the agent to lead the mission. Serrato remarks of this: "As Juni then struts into the room (an electric guitar riff of the *Spy Kids* theme music is heard), one male, unable to bridle his excitement, pumps his fist and grunts, "Yeah!" providing a moment of masculine approbation far removed from the bullying to which Juni was once subjected" (forthcoming). Carmen asks, "Where have you been all these years?" Juni responds, "I tried to strike out on my own, and I struck out." As the story unfolds, the siblings continue their tit-for-tats (including one instance when Carmen is frozen and Juni sticks his finger up her nose) as well as to become fully integrated into the story. Juni and Carmen are not pasted onto the story for the sake of placing them here; they really belong in the story in an established way. The thematic of family is organically integrated into the story that travels a full story arc that allows for the development of each of the protagonists at just the right pace.

The positive assessment as corroborated by the experience of watching a range of children with discerning taste enjoy *Spy Kids 4D* certainly does not match its critical reception. Mike Hale, for instance, considered it "visually dreary [. . .] lazily yet confusingly plotted, dominated by jokes involving vomit and an endlessly flatulent baby" (C6). In this last instance, perhaps this is an example of the mismatch of adult interpreter from child experiencing the film — its ideal audience.

THE ADVENTURES OF SHARKBOY AND LAVAGIRL IN 3-D (2005)

RODRIGUEZ CONTINUED TO SHARPEN HIS 3-D-FILM storytelling skills, bringing to life an idea—a hybrid human/ shark boy superhero—conceived by his then eight-year-old son Racer Maximiliano Rodriguez Avellán (b. 1997). Robert and his brother Marcel Rodriguez gave additional shape to Racer's story in their coauthoring of the screenplay that became the blueprint for the film. Once in Rodriguez's film-shaping hands and with a $50 million budget, his son's story about a boy raised by sharks and a girl whose touch turns into flames soon became *The Adventures of Sharkboy and Lavagirl in 3-D*. Columbia Pictures screened the film at 2,655 theaters across the country on June 10, 2005, bringing in $12.5 million on its opening weekend. It went on to make $69 million worldwide. (Only a few months before, Dimension Films released his and Frank Miller's hugely successful, award-winning neo-noir *Sin City*.)

This coming-of-age story follows the adventures of the young loner, narrator, and protagonist, Max (Cayden Boyd). He escapes everyday encounters with bullies like Linus (Jacob Davich) and marital troubles at home (parents played by David Arquette and Kristin Davis) by daydreaming—and more formally conceiving and elaborating on this daydream in his journal. Everyday objects and people become reconfigured in his daydreams and then realized in fictional form as Cookie Giants (parents), Mr. Electric (his schoolteacher), and Tobor (one of his discarded toy robots). These new entities exist in a fictional place named Planet Drool.

Max's imagination, however, is not just anchored by and extrapolated from an everyday reality. Rodriguez (and Racer Rodriguez) also invents from scratch, so to speak, the young superhero team: a boy adopted by sharks who acquires gills and a penchant for fish and becomes a martial arts master, Sharkboy (Taylor Lautner—and played by Rebel and Racer Rodriguez in a flashback sequence that portrays his early childhood) and a young girl who feels deeply misunderstood and scorches with her touch, Lavagirl (Taylor Dooley). With Mr. Electric (George Lopez, whom Rodriguez had in mind when he wrote the part) and his plughounds threatening to turn the dreamworld into a nightmare, Max and his dynamic mutant-duo fight him and Minus (the nightmare iteration of school bully Linus) on Planet Drool. Upon the advice of Tobor (scrambled anagram for "robot"), he learns to "dream a better, unselfish dream." He overcomes his fears and anxieties as he surmounts the seemingly insurmountable, including a final battle with Mr. Electric, who arrives Wizard-of-Oz style in a tornado. With the help of family and friends, Mr. Electric is vanquished, harmony is restored, and Planet Drool remains a place of dreams, not nightmares. The film ends affirming the need for dreaming and therefore creativity as well as the unity of family.

I mentioned earlier how a comic-book sensibility allows for a capacious storytelling that can and often does defy all natural and social laws. It is within this storytelling mode that we can have Thumb Thumbs, Fooglies, but also pigtails that swirl and allow little girls to fly (Gerti Giggles, for instance). It is the storytelling that follows the logic of the daydream; that is a logic whereby there are no limits to what one can do, feel, and imagine. This anything-goes sensibility that breathes life into Rodriguez's other films is literalized in *Sharkboy*.

The film's conceit is the lucid dreamscape: how children express fears and anxieties about tensions in their everyday lives, usually revolving around school and family; how lucid dreams offer limitless possibilities for rescripting dreams; how daydreams or, say, wake-dreaming can offer forms of escape and emancipation from oppressive everyday situations. Lucid dreaming activities liberate children's cognitive faculty of thinking in terms of counterfactuals and probabilities (if A, then probably B). In lucid dreams one can be aware of oneself dreaming (at a meta-diegetic remove, to use film terms) and controlling the way the story unfolds. In this sleep state, we are aware of the fact that we are the executive power that drives the dream in whatever direction we want to take it. In contrast, in nonlucid dreams the events within the dream unfold spontaneously without any orientation, direction, or control by the dreamer.

Rodriguez uses the word dream also in the sense of daydreaming. In daydreaming there are many similarities with lucid dreaming, but of course in daydreaming you are not actually asleep. At a certain point in the story Max states that he can't sleep so he has to learn to daydream. In a way, he learns to replace his sleep dreaming with an awake dreaming—or, daydreaming. He must learn to use his daydream more in the sense of the kind of creative trance that invades the artist while creating his or her work of art.

The film establishes the dream as a huge source of creativity—one that the adult world condemns or simply doesn't understand—that allows for *real action*. If the child's dream is crushed by the adults—Mr. Electric's master plan as well as the mom's condemnation of daydreaming, for instance—then so too would the imagination of the child be obliterated. The shattering of the child's capacity for dreaming would take away his or her capacity to imagine, create, and to *make new* in the world.

Max can see his world as presenting conflicts and problems. The film addresses some of the conflicts, fears, and hopes that children and tweens have. Sharkboy is separated from his father and becomes an orphan eventually raised by sharks. There is unmistakable tension between Max's parents: the mother who is characterized as a realist and the father an idealist. The statistics show that around 50% of the population of people who get married, divorce. However, Max's learning to dream a better dream allows him to imagine different outcomes, possibilities, and solutions to these problems and conflicts. This is what gives him the confidence to overcome obstacles and transform his everyday life—from vanquishing bullies at school to the uniting of family. It allows him to imagine new approaches to these problems he faces.

SHAPING DEVICES

Everybody has stories, but not all stories turn into works of art. All have images in their mind, but not all images turn into works of art, etc. Art is a shape-giving activity. Just as Faulkner had the image of a girl with muddied drawers in his mind before he could give shape to this in the form of what would become the novel *The Sound and the Fury*, so too does Racer, then Rodriguez, have an image of a Sharkboy and Lavagirl that is then given shape in stories and drawings and then in the film form.

Essentially the art of filmmaking is a shape-giving activity. Rodriguez doesn't create out of nothing—ex nihilo. With his son Racer's idea, he and Racer first imagine new shapes and new organic wholes that will bring this into existence—first as a story and drawing and then as a film. With this prime matter Rodriguez fixes for himself the goal of giving shape in the format of film to Racer's story and the drawings. He is giving them an aesthetic goal and seeks the means that would allow him to attain the goal (technical and otherwise) that is a shape-giving goal: a 3-D film. The aesthetic activity implies necessarily the work upon matter generally conceived; it implies the working on objective reality that includes dreaming, reading of comic books, viewing of films as well all other experiences in reality such as the separation of parents; it implies giving shape to anything *out there* in the world or *in there* in the mind.

As a filmmaker, Rodriguez gives shape to the idea in film form and with a specific audience in mind: that ideal audience who will understand the contents and the form that he gives to the contents; who will enjoy its colors, music, and movement—its total aesthetic as well as the story.

In addition to using the film medium to give shape to Racer's ideas, Rodriguez also chose the visual and verbal formats of young adult fiction and the children's illustrated book. These are not your usual movie tie-ins aimed at only generating money. They are carefully thought out verbal and visual re-creations of the Sharkboy and Lavagirl story. In the children's illustrated book by Robert and Racer Rodriguez *The Adventures of Sharkboy and Lavagirl: The Movie Storybook* they include only a short text alongside a more powerful presence of the images. The images acquire their full, *intended meaning* thanks to the narrative. The narrative orients the reader into how to interpret the images—images that on their own would not tell the story. Without the presence of the narrative, we would ascribe all kinds of interpretations onto the images. The images acquire their full, *intended meaning* thanks to the narrative. And yet, the images do help guide how we fill in the huge gaps left by the narrative. There is a reciprocal relationship between narrative and image.

In the young adult fiction books 1–2 (a third volume has yet to appear), by Rodriguez along with science fiction author Chris Roberson and illustrator Alex Toader (he designed characters and environments for the film as well as the *Spy Kids* films), we see how the visuals are not used to tell the young reader how to make sense of the textual information but function as a supplement to what is created in the imagination by reading the words on the page. The visuals exist as a kind of comfort for the young reader, but not as something absolutely necessary. Moreover, the sprinkle of visuals makes the job of writing more

We returned Planet Drool to its original glory. All except for Mr. Electric. He didn't want to go back to being the good electrician of the planet. He liked abusing his power. He flew back to Earth to destroy me in my sleep.

I had to finish the dream and make it real. I blinked my eyes three times (the easiest way to wake up from a dream) and I was suddenly back on Planet Earth. I got my teacher, classmates, even Linus to help stop Mr. Electric.

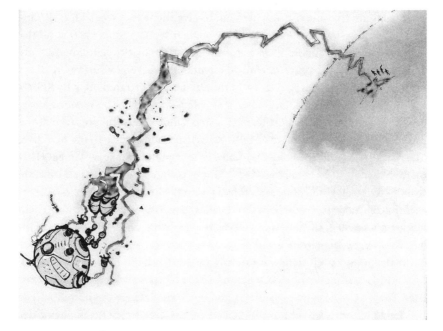

The Adventures of Sharkboy and Lavagirl: The Movie Storybook (2005) and the use of written narrative in conjunction with visual image.

efficient. Rodriguez and Roberson do not have to provide lengthy lists to detail objects and characters.

Given the centrality of the dream in this story, it is not surprising that in his shape-giving impulse Rodriguez should choose 3-D technology; with the technology and the know-how, he can realize his aesthetic goal of bringing this dream world alive and intensify the experience of dreaming for his audience. Use of 3-D along with the 1,000 visual effects created by CGI and green screen technology allow Rodriguez the possibility of diminishing the distance between the reality of the audience sitting in seats and the dream-like quality of film where the characters ride a Train of Thought or a banana-split boat down the Stream of Consciousness. Rodriguez's aim: to match as much as possible the form with the content.

The selection of the technological means for accomplishing his aesthetic goal is not the only choice Rodriguez makes. There is also the choice of what the narrator protagonist will look like. For instance, will the protagonist Max look like Racer—Latino? or not? Will the cast to play Racer's superheroes look Latino or not? (Rodriguez actually consulted Racer in his casting choices.) At this age, the bricks children, preteens, and even teens take from reality are their own direct, immediate experiences, fears, hopes, moments of joy and happiness; often the characters children invent mirror their own psychological and physiological traits. That is, the images of superheroes, for instance, are spontaneously and freshly self-centered—and I mean this in a positive way. Like gods, they tend to imagine heroes in their own image.

Perhaps it is that Rodriguez makes decisions that are not bound to such tellurian schemas precisely in his choosing to create a protagonist who is blonde and blue-eyed. Counterintuitive as it may seem, by casting the blonde, blue-eyed Cayden Boyd, Rodriguez decides to establish a strong feature of *enstrangement*, or dishabituation. To further complicate and make perceptually new (*enstrange*) the viewer's experience, the Anglo protagonist and narrator Max dreams up and imagines his superheroes as contrasts to himself: Lautner as Sharkboy and Dooley as Lavagirl appear phenotypically at least to be mixed race.

In shaping this as a story told in film form Rodriguez also decides what theme to emphasize. He clearly follows the dream conceit but also decides as the creator that the story should revolve around the importance of (1) dreams and dreaming in the education and development of the child and (2) the need to be creative, or the need to "dream a better dream, then work to make it real." Then comes all the hard work to give this shape, to ensure that all the parts cohere and constitute an organic whole as an aesthetic object, all of which of course requires the use of Rodriguez's logical (causal, counterfactual, and probabilistic) thinking and reasoning as well as focused use of memory, perception, and emotion capacities to create something new.

In many ways Rodriguez uses the storytelling format of film to get as close as possible to the essence of storytelling: film storytelling as a proximate iteration of lucid dreaming. It is this form and content that shapes the film's dreamscape envelope. It is this dreamscape container that holds and then conveys a story that operates along two oppositional poles: unity and separation. Before the story proper begins, Rodriguez offers an image of a boy with his father that conveys affection and a sense of a comforting unity. However, soon after there is a radical separation between father and son, launching the story proper. Yet, Rodriguez doesn't leave unity behind, it is simply found elsewhere: the boy creates a new family with the sharks who adopt him. He makes a best friend in Max. Then Rodriguez introduces yet another rupture with the arrival of Lavagirl, who becomes friends with Sharkboy, taking Max's new best friend away. Then Lavagirl, Sharkboy, and Max become a unity.

The story moves back and forth between these poles of unity and rupture—two of the central preoccupations of children with family and friends and often expressed in dream form. As the story unfolds, this generative motor of unity and disharmony continues to express itself, but in the oppositional pairs: light and dark. The trio must travel to the Dream Lair to stop dreams from malfunctioning—to stop darkness from spreading on Planet Drool and the earth. The seed of the story is unity followed by rupture between light and darkness. Darkness is conceived of as the malfunctioning of dreams. Lightness is conceived of as the harmonious working of dreams and the unity of family and friends.

The story writ large, then, is about how darkness—the selfishness, solipsism, and narcissism of parent and teacher figures like Mr. Electric/Mr. Electricidad and the mom as well as bullies like Minus/Linus—threatens to spread to destroy lightness—the unity and harmony represented by Max and his friendship with Sharkboy and Lavagirl as well as with his father. The key to the story: to overcome this anguish, this state of disquiet caused by rupture of unity of father and son, is to dream better dreams that are not solipsistic in content but that reach out to the collective in a positive way.

Dreaming and daydreaming change the way Max sees things, giving him courage and energy precisely because he sees that things can be different. Through dreaming activity a child like Max can liberate his cognitive faculty of thinking in terms of counterfactuals, seeing the different outcomes, possibilities, and solutions to problems and conflicts. This is what gives audacity, confidence to try new things in the world. Through the daydreaming, he exercises his counterfactual and probabilistic reasoning, allowing him to change the position from which he sees things with respect to the real world. This gives impulse and energy to his desire for change.

Sharkboy offers children in the audience the possibility of vicariously experiencing this heuristic trial-and-error exploration—all within safe circumstances where they won't be harmed. Max's dreaming is a harmless form of trial and error. And the children in the audience can also experience this within the comfort of the cinema. Max realizes that his dreams don't have to be negative and menacing; they don't have to lead to nightmarish dead ends. He realizes that dreams can be worked upon and that he can control them as lucid dreams, creating whatever outcome he wants in the dream world.

SHORTS (2009)

JUST AS RACER'S IDEAS AND STORIES WERE THE BUILDing blocks Rodriguez reorganized in the making of *The Adventures of Sharkboy and Lavagirl in 3-D*, so too does his son Rebel's idea (b. 1999) of a wishing rock told in the style of *The Little Rascals* become the conceit for what would be known as *Shorts*. (Many of the other ideas in the film came from the mind of another of Robert Rodriguez's family members, cousin Alvaro Rodriguez—credited as a cowriter. They include, for instance, the parents' dilemma, the Black Box, Carbon, Helvetica and Cole ["Coal"], Toe and Nose, and Mr. Noseworthy, among others.) Distributed by Warner Brothers, the film opened August 21, 2009, on 3,105 screens across the country. Along with three assistant directors, coeditor Ethan Maniquis, and co-composers George Oldiziey and Carl Thiel, Rodriguez gave shape to Rebel's idea for $20 million. It brought in $29 million in worldwide ticket sales; it received mixed critical reviews, commenting mostly on its ineffectual use of slapstick and its predictable story line.

Again, Rodriguez makes certain formal (technical) and content (character, actor, setting, theme, plot) choices when turning Rebel's idea into a script and then a film story. (Alvaro Rodriguez also worked on the script.) He also keeps in mind that the choices should add up to an artistic whole that will tickle the fancy of a specific audience—an audience that largely matches the age group (a little above and below) of the tween protagonists. He chooses to set the story in a suburban community that he calls "Black Falls." He chooses to make this a modern-day company town where all the families essentially seem to work for

Black Box Industries, owned by Mr. Carbon Black (James Spader). He chooses to create a singular narrating entity, Toby "Toe" Thompson (Jimmy Bennett) to act as the glue that holds a variety of vignettes, or shorts, together.

Shorts is about different individuals discovering the wishing rock (as it turns out, it's a sentient entity from another planet) and their making either banal, idiotic, or narcissistic wishes that come true. In the end, the wishing rock grows weary of these demands, threatening to destroy the world. However, as with his other children-oriented films, Rodriguez chooses to move from moments of disunity to a final thematic center-staging of the importance of the unity of family and of community. It is in the power of the collective that the town and its inhabitants restore harmony.

Rodriguez chooses to give this shape using the conceit of the DVD fast-forward, play, pause, and rewind functions. As Toby introduces each of the shorts, he also controls the images the audience sees. As the story unfolds, he occasionally gets ahead of himself in the telling and the showing, so he backtracks and rewinds. As such, Toby is the master of ceremonies, controlling what we see and hear in the story, even what the camera proper sees and hears as it tells the story. That is, Rodriguez chooses to playfully expose the device (or break the fourth wall, in Brecht's terminology), reminding the viewer that we are watching something that is artificially constructed, a story told in the film format that reorganizes the building blocks of reality: from genres of science fiction to corporate exploitation and the presence of germophobes and boogers in the world. Yet, Rodriguez also attunes to the way children (and adults) increasingly consume stories in film format—first as VHS and then as DVDs whereby you can play, pause, rewind, and fast-forward a film. He chooses to foreground this film-viewing technology that informs how most families now consume film media: at home with a remote control.

Of course, Rodriguez's foregrounding of this doesn't aim for a Brechtian

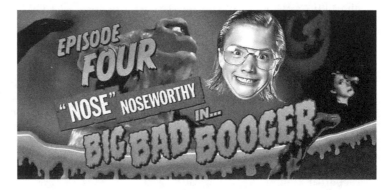

Shorts (2009). Title panel for Episode Four.

Shorts (2009). A booger transforms into a larger-than-life-sized monster.

moment of sociopolitical clarity. It's simply there to add to the fun of watching the different characters handle the consequences of their different wishes. Moreover, the wishes themselves allow Rodriguez to introduce the comic-book sensibility within the content along with elements that make up the grotesque. Toby has matchbox-sized rascally aliens help him get through encounters with bullies Colbert "Cole" (Devon Gearhart) and sister Helvetica "Hel" Black (Jolie Vanier). Loogie (Trevor Gagnon) and his companions Laser (Leo Howard) and Lug (Rebel Rodriguez) end up with crocodiles snapping and snakes biting at their toes; Loogie even sprouts a telephone from his head. "Nose" Noseworthy (Jake Short) inadvertently wishes one of his boogers into gigantesque existence. Toby's parents become attached literally to one another like Siamese twins.

In form and content, Rodriguez creates a film that is coherent in its aesthetic aims and goals. Its comic-book and grotesque sensibility captures well the preoccupations and imagination of a tween audience. Arguably, however, when the end comes and harmony is restored, it feels as if this is lost and an adult-like worldview becomes omnipresent—one that imagines, even if playfully, the parents coming together by practicing yoga (and not text messaging), Carbon Black turning a new leaf as philanthropist and not capitalist, and Toby concluding: "Be sure you're worth wishing for."

Tour de Noir *Comic-Book Film*

W HILE FILMMAKERS HAD SHOWN AN INTEREST IN adapting to the silver screen the graphic novel *Sin City* (1991–2000), none had succeeded in convincing its author/artist, Frank Miller. Miller had been stung on film adaptations of his *Daredevil* and *Electra* comics, and, well, he just didn't consider it possible to make a live-action version of the highly stylized *Sin City*. Until, that is, Rodriguez flew Miller down to his Troublemaker Studios to screen a short episode (later used as the film's opening vignette, "The Customer Is Always Right") he had made using his Sony HD cameras, CGI and animatic software tools, and a requisite thirty-foot green screen. Miller was floored. With Miller on board as codirector and a production budget of $40 million, Rodriguez created one of the most aesthetically significant of comic book re-creations.

It happened that it was also a critical and commercial success. With the Weinstein brothers' Dimension Films distribution, it was released on April 1, 2005, pulling in $29 million its opening weekend. It went on to make $158 million at the box office worldwide as well as to pick up many accolades, including the Cannes Film Festival's Technical Grand Prize award.

The idea to re-create *Sin City* had been long in the stewing. Following closely the comic book as it was published during the 1990s, Rodriguez was drawn to Miller's intense, kinetic visual- and verbal-expressive storytelling style. Already during this period, he had begun thinking about making a film re-creation. At one point, he remarks how he considered the comic the "best shot, written, directed, lit, and edited movie that people have never seen, just on paper" (16). (See his and Miller's *Frank Miller's Sin City*.) That he would not be able to clear a schedule to make the film till the 2000s worked in his favor. Simply speaking, 35mm film technology would not have worked. It could only be the digital advances in filmmaking technology that would allow for the shaping of the graphic novel into a film. Having mastered digital shooting and postproduction visual effects technology with films such as *Spy Kids 2*, *Spy Kids 3*, and *Once Upon a Time in Mexico*, he could take on a project such as this in a way that would at once remain faithful to Miller's stylization and make it new *as a film*. As Emily R. Anderson remarks of his use of digital technology, "much of the film is actually *drawn*, albeit with pixels instead of pens. In this sense, the film is much closer to a graphic narrative than any film shot on location or on a traditional sound stage could be" (forthcoming).

From the beginning, Rodriguez knew that while he had the filmmaking expertise, he would need Miller's eyes and ears on the set to be sure the tone, rhythm, movement, sound, and look were accurate. That is, Rodriguez wanted this to be a Frank Miller film as much as, if not more than, his own. In fact, a week into the making of the film, the Directors Guild of America informed him that a codirectorship credit would violate DGA rules. While they granted waivers to filmmaking teams such as Larry (now Lana) and Andy Wachowski and Albert and Allen Hughes, they would not do the same for Rodriguez and Miller. To do the right thing and give Miller codirector credit, he resigned from the DGA knowing well that this would cut him off from work with its affiliate studios.

Of course, there have been other aesthetically noteworthy comic-book adaptations such as Christopher Nolan's *Batman* trilogy (2005–2012), inspired by Miller's noir-styled reboot of the superhero. Nolan's films do not aspire in any way to replicate the comic book visually. Others like Mario Bava's *Diabolik* (1968), Warren Beatty's *Dick Tracy* (1990), Christian Volckman's *Renaissance* (2006), and certain sequences of Ang Lee's *The Hulk* (2003) do seek in their aesthetic aims and goals to *look* like the comic book. One way or another, they don't succeed; something is lost in the move from the comic book to the film storytelling medium; the attempt at a one-to-one translation of the static panels of comic books or comic strips into the motion-photographic medium of live-action film one way or another has resulted in products that unwittingly tip into the realm of camp or the tedious.

Rodriguez does succeed in re-creating the abstract visual style, kinetic rhythm, and expressive noir tone seen in the mean streets of Miller's volumes *Hard Good Bye*, *Big Fat Kill*, and *Yellow Bastard*. In a review for *Sight & Sound*, Kim Newman remarks of comic-book adaptations that have tried to look like comic books, "none has so successfully seemed like a gloss on the originals as *Sin City*" ("Sin City" 72). Rodriguez didn't want to make a Rodriguez film, but to make a Miller film—therefore to turn a comic book into a film, and not to adapt a comic book into film. That is, his aesthetic goals were to transform a comic book into a film and not to use the comic book as an excuse to make a film. The Rodriguez/Miller result: a *re*-creation that stands on its own, but that captures perfectly the original comic book.

Several scholars have commented on this move from one to another medium—or, Rodriguez's intent to make a *Miller film*. Erin Eighan considers how Rodriguez's move from comic book to film format turns the film into a "hybridized medium—one that bridges the continuous motion of film with the panels and gutters of comics, the human face with caricature, the sound with silence" (forthcoming). Patrick Colm Hogan considers *Sin City* to be in the tradition of the painterly film—the film that is drawn over by paint to alter the film, evaluating its value less in the adaptation quality (does it succeed in translating the original or not) but rather in "the creativity of the filmmaker" that is enhanced by the "integration of knowledge across diverse areas that are not commonly integrated" (forthcoming). In a specific analysis of several shots Emily R. Anderson notes how Rodriguez uses his knowledge of the different technological means for storytelling (film photograph vs. comic book page) to create a likeness to the comic book panel's framing and composition by using his monitor to compare "the image he was capturing to the relevant panels in Miller's book. He could thus adjust the camera and actors to correspond to the panels" (forthcoming).

Rodriguez/Miller work with original comic-book material that follows a series of moody, lone heroic figures (Marv and Dwight) who cross ethical lines to protect the weak, innocent, and exploited in a world filled with unimaginably corrupt and amoral police, politicians, and clerics; Miller's authority figures all spring from the same dysfunctional family line—one that spawns pedophiles and cannibals. Drawn to the noir storytelling format, Miller sought to use this as his generic envelope. The crime/noir genre is essentially a morality tale, but with a twist: the heroes would do whatever it takes to serve and protect. Moreover, it was a genre that seemed appropriate to reflect the present day (and the time of the story proper) whereby Miller considered the social fabric itself ripping apart at the seams. He remarks, "Times of great stress are clarifying times, and the crime genre, because it is so much about good and evil, delves so deeply into evil.[. . .] It is also a motif of crime fiction—a la Chandler, or Spillane, or Hammet—that these characters are disguised. They look like dirty knights. They don't let on that most of them are compulsive do-gooders" (Rodriguez and Miller, *Frank Miller's Sin City* 12).

Miller's comics, of course, up the ante on the noir genre. He exaggerates and intensifies characters' traits and the hermitic, closed-world feel found in yesteryear's noir genre. He stylizes and abstracts visually the black/white noir conceit. And, he uses squares, rectangles, and crisscrossed lines of black and white to convey a relentless sense of confinement and claustrophobia felt by his flawed heroes. By remaking the comic as a film, Rodriguez/Miller ask that the present-day filmgoer be moved by the aesthetic experience; they also ask that the filmgoer step into an earlier 1950s epoch, but to experience this through the lens of a socially disintegrating and destructive present-day world with fewer and fewer options.

FRANKENSTEINS

Rodriguez/Miller's *Sin City* is a re-creation and recomposition in the best sense. They do not try to reproduce their individual and idiosyncratic experiences of every panel of the comic book. Rather, they seek to reproduce a distillation of the plot and of the aesthetic goals and means behind the creation of the original work and its re-creation in their mind. Not to crush the development of the story and for it to stand on its own as a new, original product, Rodriguez/Miller distill into paraphrase form their experiences of the comic book, then rebuild them in film form as a series of aesthetic patterns I identify throughout this book as the grotesque.

Importantly, Rodriguez/Miller re-create—and don't seek to imitate in making the film. Imitation would assume some type of one-to-one correspondence with the original and with the reality *behind* the original. This is not the case. In goals and aims, *Sin City* the film doesn't imitate anything out there in nature. Rodriguez/Miller use the bricks of reality, including other products such as Spillane novels or rebel films, but reorganize them in new and novel ways. The film is like a Frankenstein monster—a composite shape created by Rodriguez/Miller based on something out in the world (the comic book most visibly). That is, they keep in mind that the making of the film is an aesthetic artifact that adds to the world. In this sense, while Rodriguez/Miller employ all variety of digital abracadabra special effects in the making of *Sin City*, it is no different than a Nicholas Ray's making new with his realist film, *Rebel Without a Cause* (1955). Both are recompositions of bricks of reality that create in their totality something new in the world.

I offer this seemingly high-minded and abstract conceptualizing of Rodriguez/Miller's re-creation to point us in the right direction for engaging and appreciating the film. To *really* appreciate *Sin City*, the filmgoer has to get rid of all aesthetic prejudices, that common *doxa* that art *is* imitation of reality. *Sin City* is a very successful work of art. It should be judged as such; it should be experienced as a new creation that adds to the world—a creation in which two central brains (along with a huge crew of other creative brains) gather to work to create this new product. If we stick to the idea of its being an imitation, we will only ever have a very elementary approach to the film, losing sight of the instruments needed to analyze and judge the film.

An audience familiar with the comic book will recognize that Rodriguez/Miller's distillation and then recomposition of the original chose to create a strong sense of a formal parallel between the film and the comic book. Rodriguez/Miller use the dominant black-and-white schema of the comic book. However, through various digital means that allow for the multiple layering of the film, they make vitally new this black/white schema by introducing carefully calibrated splashes of very defined, intense color: red lipstick, blue eyes, fluorescent-like white blood, and golden locks, for instance.

Working with a visual and auditory media necessarily means that Rodriguez/Miller must make other choices when distilling then recompositing. In some re-creations, it is a matter of careful mise-en-scène composition and lens choice. Emily R. Anderson remarks of the scene with Marv waking up next to Goldie who is dead: "Even the difference in aspect ratio between the images is smoothed over with the apparent use of a wider lens in the film, allowing the walls to take up more space in the frame. Rodriguez managed this similarity in framing and composition by comparing, on his monitor, the image he was capturing to the relevant panels in Miller's book. He could thus adjust the camera and actors to correspond to the panels" (forthcoming). In other instances, it is a question of re-creating in the voice-over what appears marginalized in the sidebar. In the original comic book, Miller uses the margins as a kind of sidebar where Marv's voice-over is read, and often, too, as a bridge between incongruously juxtaposed panels.

For those familiar with the comic book, Miller pushes the readers/viewers to work hard in their gap filling (imagining) as they move from one panel to another. He uses clear-cut, very well-defined lines, but minimally so; raindrops can appear as very thick veils that don't allow the readers/viewers to see clearly the features of the bodies portrayed. He contrasts this with heavy blocks and silhouettes. These also work to abstract and stylize the figures and their movement. Indeed, Miller uses the interior monologues to help guide us from one abstract panel to the next.

Rodriguez/Miller do not choose to use bubbles, text boxes, margins, or sidebars in the film, of course. Rather, they choose not to try to translate such conventions from one format to the next. Rather, they use the auditory channel for a voice-over narration that establishes the noir mood—and interiority of its protagonists, John Hartigan (Bruce Willis), Marv (Mickey Rourke), and Dwight (Clive Owen). We discover that Hartigan is likely the only straight-up cop on the beat and that he's also conflicted about his love for the girl he saved from being raped but who has grown up, Nancy Callahan (Jessica Alba); we discover that Marv is more than a thuggish lout—longing for companionship

Sin City (2005). Comic book panel and film
shot of Dwight (Clive Owen) and Gail
(Rosario Dawson).

and love, he avenges the death of a prostitute, Goldie (Jaime King), he'd fallen
in love with; his actions lead to his death by electric chair; and we discover that
Dwight is less self-centered and sexist than seen at first blush, willing to die de-
fending the exploited and oppressed women of Old Town.

Rodriguez/Miller choose to use real actors to depict the comic book characters. However, with the careful use of contrasts of light and dark (even lighting a face in counterintuitive ways, such as with two light sources hitting Clive
Owen's cheeks, as can be seen in this photograph), they convey a similar stylized effect. As Emily R. Anderson remarks, "Rodriguez was able to light his
actors, often using just a key light and a backlight, without regard for light
spill—the light that would illuminate not only the actor but the set as well.
Rodriguez wanted the set to remain dark, and because the "set" was merely a
graphic created in postproduction it could be as dark as he liked, as dark as in
Miller's panels. The result is a film that, far more than most black-and-white
films, is actually black and white, but that still manages to separate the figures
from their environment" ("*Sin City*, Style, and the Status of Noir" forthcoming). Of course, while highly constructed and with a very specific look that

achieves a specific aesthetic affect, the film does not achieve the same level of abstraction and stylization as the drawn comic. Moreover, when it comes to depictions of violence (cannibalism, for instance) and naked bodies (Lucille's breasts, for instance), Miller can do in the comic book what Rodriguez/Miller can't do in the film — for commercial reasons, certainly.

Even though highly stylized, the comic book can portray the raw violence and sensuality in ways that would be considered scandalous in a live-action (albeit highly stylized) film. As postproduction visual effects supervisor Keefe Boerner discusses, even though the film is still very violent, the visual effects make it more palatable: "If you really watched somebody stab swords into heads or cutting hands off, it would be too gross and there would be no way for us to show that in the theatre. But the fact that the blood isn't red and it glows white makes the scene more palatable.[. . .] The MPAA basically said that we would have had to cut many scenes if the movie had been in color, but because the film is in black and white we can get away with more graphic violence" (*Frank Miller's Sin City* 25).

NEW FRONTIERS

Whether it was his early use of VHS technology to film and edit films or his discovery of HD filmmaking technology, Rodriguez has always been one to seek out the technical means to open audiences to new film frontiers. He had long been attracted to the work of Ralph Bakshi; Bakshi is perhaps best known for his drawn-over live-action animation *Fire and Ice* (1983); this was a kind of proto-motion-capture/rotoscope film that used real-life actors who would be traced over in postproduction. (At the time of writing this book, Rodriguez was working on a recreation of *Fire and Ice* — a glimpse of which I was lucky to catch during my visit to the Troublemaker Studios.) With the advances in interface technology between computers and digital film cameras, Rodriguez could step up to the challenge of making a film of Miller's stylized comic book. Working closely with his Troublemaker digital previsualization art crew, he could use software animatics to see a blueprint of the entire film before the shooting itself, saving time (and therefore money) during production in the choreographing of the actors as well as the setting up of the camera angles. While few physical sets were built (the bar and Shellie's, played by Brittany Murphy, apartment) and the green screen was used ninety-nine percent of the time, Rodriguez/Miller decided to use "real" guns, ropes, window frames, doorways, the bar, and cars as points of reference for the actors — and also eventually the audience. They knew well that this would give the actors something tangible to feel, point, or drive, say; that is, they knew that the objects would enhance and fill out in the actors'

Sin City (2005). *Image of Brittany Murphy as Shellie
leaning out a real window with a green screen backdrop.*

minds how they were to move through an otherwise completely empty space; how they would imagine their acting not as with or against another actor sometimes (with green screen technology, actors that share a frame could be filmed in isolation from one another and at different times) or a stage set filled with objects, structures, and the like. As actor Bruce Willis remarks of the experience:

> The best way I could describe the sound stage would be like working on a Playhouse 90 set.[...] There was a real dock, there was a real staircase, the cars were all real, the props were real; other than that it all had to be imagined. It was all just a big green stage.[...] In that kind of acting, you really have to rely on a certain amount of sense memory.[...] You have to know what you want to do with the character. I rely a lot on both Robert and Frank. (*Frank Miller's Sin City* 217)

The previsualization design and postproduction digital technology allow Rodriguez/Miller not only to reduce the time of the shoot—Willis comments how his part would normally have taken six weeks, but it only took ten days—but to stylize the film in ways that capture the feel of the original. To stylize the appearance of blood, they used fluorescent red liquid and hit it with a black light, allowing them to turn the blood very white in postproduction. The technology also presented certain challenges. For instance, the yellow color of Roark Junior (Nick Stahl) didn't react well with the green screen; he had to be painted blue and then in postproduction colored yellow (for more on the techniques used, see Ashcraft). They can modify the movement of the car (real prop set in front of a green screen) in ways that at once make it appear as if it's going fast and yet not at all as if a comic book panel. They make the action (the violence, car chases, and the like) *new* by setting the goal of making a film within a genre that will take that genre to a new level.

The overall effect, much like the comic book, allows Miller/Rodriguez to make *new* our sensations, thoughts, and feelings. It allows them to immerse the filmgoer in a storyworld that is, in a way, in between the real and drawn—but always conceived from beginning to end as existing within the realm of the comic book. (This differs from films like Richard Linklater's *A Scanner Darkly*, where the actors are drawn over and our brains are constantly looking for the real behind the animation; this technique, I would argue, doesn't allow for full stimulation of the imagination; we never fully submerge ourselves in Linklater's story; it always feels artificial to a distracting degree.)

I mentioned earlier how Miller uses the interior monologue of his protagonists as a kind of sound (in the mind) bridge between the panels. Rodriguez/Miller use the voice-over in this way as well as extradiegetic music. Along with Graeme Revell and John Debney (Debney worked on the first *Spy Kids* films), they create a sound design that fits with each of the three chapters (Hard Goodbye, The Big Fat Kill, and That Yellow Bastard) that make up the film. The chapters (each also with their own respective visual effects teams) each have their own music motifs. This also functions to bridge the different spaces and give direction to our sense-making capacities—we know we are still in chapter X and not in chapter Y. For instance, for the first chapter, Miller/Rodriguez sought to create a noir *and* modern sound, so Rodriguez used a modified saxophone to give a twisting, subterranean, dark, moody–nostalgic feel to the sound; he added tonal shifts when necessary to intensify the sound's disquieting effect. In addition, they deformed the traditional film-noir score using guitars, detuned saxophones (tenor, tuned-down baritone, and bass) to act as a kind of glue in the audience's mind that would hold all three chapters together as a whole; they introduce this thematic sound with the opening and the opening credits and as a tone that plays throughout the film. (See Allina.)

OTHER INGREDIENTS

The technical wizardry comes alive, of course, in the hands of the choreographing of the actors, but not just any actors. In fact, Rodriguez had already picked out his A-list of actors when he screened the vignette example to lasso Miller; he included the lineup as part of the vignette's credit list. As a director whom actors enjoy working with—and whose film productions do not swallow up time—he was able to get his wish list of talent. In fact, he used that same three-minute vignette to attract the actor talent to the production. He had already worked with several of the actors such as Josh Hartnett and Elijah Wood in *The Faculty*, Carla Gugino from the *Spy Kids* franchise, and Danny Trejo from the Mariachi trilogy, for instance. Others were new. In all cases, Miller/Rodriguez managed to bring out (and perhaps in spite of the green screen technology, where you have an actor working against the grain by fighting or talking to thin air) the best in their acting capacities and qualities.

The film is also totally iconoclastic. We invest emotionally in stereotypical ways in the main characters. We really hate the guys that we are supposed to dislike. We feel good when the "good" guys wipe the bad guys clean off the face of the earth. However, the film also gives the audience enough time to establish the psychological makeup of each of the protagonists, so that even though they may be singular in aims and obsessions, we care about their accomplishing their goals as well as feel deeply for their suffering of huge psychological torment. We care about the fact that they are single-handedly (in the name of fairness and justice) battling very powerful men who are at the top, the pinnacle of these extremely powerful institutions of the state: judicial, religious, political, coercive branches. We care also that the protagonists are unwilling to yield to corruption, fighting to the end (death, usually) to uphold some sense of right and wrong. This is why we find exciting a simple car chase: it can end with the death of the protagonist we are rooting for or its opposite. This is why film and comics scholar Jared Gardner identifies how the film, with all the prosthetics and digital tools, turns actors into "graphic icons, capable of absorbing bullets and the anxieties of their audience" (185).

Within this iconoclasm, Miller/Rodriguez make new in unexpected ways: in the choice to turn an otherwise Anglo-inhabited (WASP or Irish, mostly) storyworld into one with a Latina presence. Latina actress Jessica Alba is cast in the central female role, Nancy Callahan; and Rosario Dawson is cast as the badass prostitute, Gail. Alba and Dawson come with their own nuanced adjectival baggage: the lighter-skinned Alba is often cast in ethnically nondescript roles, and the darker-skinned Dawson in ethnically marked, urban roles. (For more on this see the work of Mary Beltrán.) Miller/Rodriguez put front and center the Latinoness of the characters. Moreover, they don't follow politically correct procedures generally of inhibiting women's look and movement. They depict women as composites of opposites and all in between: tough and sensual, smart and affectionate.

As I mentioned earlier, we must approach *Sin City* as a re-creation that adds something new to the world. If one doesn't and we follow an imitation approach to it (the misguided common doxa concerning art generally), then one might dismiss the film for being too misogynistic, for instance. It would mean not assessing the film on its own terms as an aesthetic artifact that refers to the building blocks of reality (we recognize people and objects, feelings and thoughts) but rearranges these blocks to make something radically new: a highly stylized world where the ugly (Rourke transformed with prosthetics and makeup) and the beautiful (Gugino, Alba, Dawson, for instance) comingle and without any ideological constraints—political correctness or otherwise.

COMIC-BOOK FILM APOTHEOSIS

Within the constraint of re-creating the graphic novel, Rodriguez/ Miller set themselves an aesthetic goal—and global vision—whereby all the elements that make up each segment will add up to the whole. The result is an aesthetic success. To achieve this success, as already mentioned in passing, requires not only the close collaboration of Rodriguez with Miller, but also the harnessing and orchestrating of the work and creativity of many mini-minds, if you will. The list of people mentioned in the end credits is astounding. From the previsualization arts crew to the postproduction digital effects teams at Troublemaker Studios and elsewhere, including Hybride in Canada, *Sin City*'s aesthetic success illustrates the importance of the orchestra–conductor nature of a director (or, in this case, directors). *Sin City* gives testament to the fact that one can obtain logical coherence and an aesthetic balance and harmony through the contributions of the many people involved.

The successful transposition of comic book into film in *Sin City* includes this paradoxical conveying of the stillness of the panels and the action we imagine in the gutters in between as we move from panel to panel; the film conveys well how movement and action are seemingly the sole reason for the motive, or the motor of the stories, in both film and comic book. As the story unfolds, this movement and action become (like the comic) more and more abstract and stylized; the shots increase that depict square and rectangle shapes filling up the mise-en-scène; just as the comic conveys a world that is increasingly fragmented and confining, so too does the film in its visual composition, acting, and rhythm. Yet, just as the film achieves this, Miller/Rodriguez bring to our visual experience, in Jared Gardner's words, a "remarkable stillness" (185). Gardner continues, "The dedication to Miller's framing becomes for Rodriguez an excuse to move away from the kinetic drive from frame to frame (whose force is to erase the frame), focusing on the static image, the graphic. For all its kinetic energy and ultraviolent action, the film comes as close as any other to translating onto the screen the effect of the gutter, of the frame, of the plastic icon" (186).

In other words, this is the most *comic book* of comic-book films because it knows well that it is working in another medium, and not trying to force a one-to-one transposition. As Emily R. Anderson writes, "were Rodriguez to 'translate' Miller in the most limited sense — adding 150,000 drawings and screening them at 24 per second — he would be forsaking everything that is valuable in the remediation. Instead, he locates his film in the history of the medium with the constant references to film production and conventions, conventions he flouts or adheres to in unmotivated succession. Indeed, even the similarities between Rodriguez's text and Miller's are experiments in what film is capable of — whether it can violate the physical laws of light and shadow, for example, or of color and tone" (forthcoming). Finally, I turn to the words of Miller himself: "*Sin City* is far and away the most faithful translation of a comic book to film, and we're finding that a lot of things that filmmakers have often said can't translate from comics, the particular kind of dialogue, the very abrupt jump cutting — from image to image, and from moment to moment — sure seems to edit out nice" (Miller and Rodriguez 12).

Otherworldly Mutants, Bandidas, Borderland Vigilantes … Fight Back

*P*LANET TERROR WAS A FILM LONG IN THE MAKING. Rodriguez first thought of creating a zombie flick during the production of *The Faculty* (1998) when he roughed out thirty pages of a script. He had a feeling the zombie genre as a cinematic trend would rise from the dead. As he predicted, the genre did become popular once again. However, Rodriguez was arm-deep in the making of many other films, least of which were of the walking-dead variety. It would not be till the making of *Sin City* that he would be able to entertain the possibility of making a zombie flick. If he were to do it, he wanted it to be as part of a B-movie double feature. He wanted it to have a distinctive presence by generating the feel of an earlier era of experiencing films—a grindhouse double feature. He knew the other half of the equation could only be Tarantino—his equal when it came to the singular wish to entertain audiences. For some time, Rodriguez and Tarantino had been collecting grindhouse film prints such as *They Call Her One Eye* (1973); *Rolling Thunder* (1977); *The Glory Stompers* (1967); *Dirty Mary, Crazy Larry* (1974); *Jackson County Jail* (1976); *Bucktown* (1975); *Ghetto Freaks* (1970); *Freebie and the Bean* (1974); *The Lady in Red* (1979); and *White Lightning* (1973). Over a period of a year, ideas passed between Tarantino and Rodriguez, making it clear that Rodriguez's part of the double bill would be his zombie flick. They wanted their respective films to shift genre gears during the viewing experience; this happens midway through *Planet Terror* and Tarantino's *Death Proof*.

Backing Rodriguez and Tarantino's twenty-first-century resuscitation of the grindhouse exploitation double-bill experience, the Weinstein brothers' Dimension Films released *Grindhouse: Planet Terror* and *Death Proof* on April 6,

2007. *Grindhouse* was released to critical applause. Peter Travers remarked of Rodriguez's digital shooting that he "keeps his camera on the run, and you can feel him flying from the sheer glee of it" and goes on to state of *Death Proof* that it "bubbles over with rich, juicy chunks of Quentinese, a Niagara of bravado, camaraderie, sex talk, pop-culture references and aching vulnerability." And audiences loved the *Grindhouse* double-bill experience. Some even told Rodriguez it was "the best night at the movies ever." However, because of a failed marketing campaign that included only small monies spent on advertising, few knew about the film before and during its release. This cost the film its well-deserved audiences and, of course, money. On its opening weekend, the double feature took in $11.6 million with the total cost of the two films in the $53 million range. In international ticket sales it went on to make $67 million. (This does not include DVD sales.)

TECHNIQUE

Rodriguez used his tried and true digital filmmaking tools to make *Planet Terror*. (Given his budget track record and use of digital technology, Rodriguez's film was by far the less expensive of the *Grindhouse* double bill.) With the growing of the digital wing of Troublemaker Studios, Rodriguez and his team of visual effects artists, 2-D compositing artists and assistants, and research and concept development crew could create a layout and then create, with previsualization 3-D animation software, an animatic of the whole. And state-of-the-art technology like the Wacom tablet and Adobe After Effects soft-

Planet Terror (2007). Image of Cherry with green painted cast to match up with the green screen for postproduction CGI *special effects.*

Planet Terror (2007). *Image of Cherry with digitally created machine-gun leg.*

ware allowed Rodriguez and his team to be able to draw an image from the script that would then be uploaded as a digitized image to be animated. Rodriguez's 2-D storyboard artist Mark Baird talks about this process and how he would "always try to give a little bit more [...] to make the scene entertaining" to the filmgoer (*Grindhouse* 89). The animatic would be played on a video monitor alongside the HD camera and its monitor. This would save time during the production and allow for a certain scheduling flexibility for bringing in actors for the shoot. With this in-house digital technology, too, while in production Rodriguez could add or change a scene remarkably fast.

It is this technology that allowed Rodriguez once again to push the envelope in terms of giving shape to his ideas—both at the level of the form (the film's grindhouse texture and appearance) and content (Cherry's machine-gun appendage). To achieve the grindhouse look of the film, digital artists (Rodney Brunet, Chris Olivia, Alex Toader) added a flutter, fingerprint blurs, scratches, and flashes to the frames—especially in places where the grindhouse film reels traditionally would be most damaged: the heads and tails that were damaged most because of the mechanics of editing and projecting.

At the same time, the feel and look needed to be integrated into the total aesthetic. Rodriguez wanted the feel of the grindhouse to be more emphasized at certain points of the story than in others. It appears, for instance, most scratched and damaged when the bedroom scene between El Wray (Freddy Rodriguez) and Cherry (Rose McGowan) gets too hot and heavy, conveying the effect of the film reel's being burned by the projector lamp. (See Rodriguez's book with Tarantino, *Grindhouse*.)

The use of digital technology also allowed for a great freedom of expression within the film's content. Rodriguez can show a zombie chewing off Cherry's leg and then later Cherry's walking stilt-like with a prosthetic wooden table leg only to exchange this for a machine-gun/grenade-launching peg leg—a weapon she wields with great agility, making use of one of her "useless" talents as a go-go dancer.

REEL ELEMENTS

Not all is digital visual effect in the film. In fact, there are more real, physical sets here than in some of the earlier films that also employ a heavy use of digital technology. And of course Rodriguez chooses to use real actors. Again, however, the use of digital technology frees up his choices in terms of whom he can cast. With the whole film laid out in animatics, he can bring in the actor on his or her schedule for the shots needed. In postproduction, it all fits together to make a whole.

As with his other films, he chooses to work with familiar and unfamiliar actors; with knowns and unknowns. He casts pop singer Stacy Ferguson as Tammy, the lesbian love-interest of Dakota (Marley Shelton); she doesn't last long before the zombies literally scoop her brains out from the back of her head. Jeff Fahey plays the redneck, BBQ "Bone Shack" owner, JT. He brings back Tom Savini (*From Dusk till Dawn*) as a buffoon-like deputy; he also has Michael Parks reprise his role as Earl McGraw. And he casts well-knowns such as Freddy Rodriguez as El Wray, who drives a wrecking truck but has some kind of special ops training; Bruce Willis is cast as Lieutenant Muldoon, who guards a vaccine that controls the virus, which they breathe to stop explosive boils from breaking out; this is the film's sci-fi infusion. Rose McGowan plays the go-go dancer Cherry, trying to make a new life. Naveen Andrews is cast as a testicle-collecting mad scientist, Abby; Josh Brolin, as the sociopath, Dr. William Block; and Quentin Tarantino, as a would-be rapist soldier; when he attempts to rape Cherry, his penis mutates into a dripping fountain of pus.

Rodriguez gives his audience a sea of characters to follow. However, his process of writing the script and casting helps give each character a unique sensibility. He would write a character up to a point, cast the actor, and then finish writing the character. Instead of having a script that's finished from A–Z, he writes enough for an impressionistic image that is filled in once the actor is cast. Ultimately, this allowed him to create a very idiosyncratic cast of characters who express startlingly idiosyncratic behaviors and idiolects; each speaks in his or her own voice in a very distinctive way, infusing characteristics that distinguish one from the other, as well as adding richness and texture to an otherwise pretty simple plot and otherwise repetitive series of explosions and gunfire.

Rodriguez is careful not to rely just on the shift in generic convention that happens midway through the film (from zombie to sci-fi mode), but to use the actors and the comingling of their very varied social positions and idiolect registers to intersperse the scenes of fighting and explosions. While some of the fight sequences are startling and innovative, if it were not for Rodriguez's careful integration of the character scenes (each character expresses his or her idiosyncratic worldview), they might have felt repetitive and monotonous. And Rodriguez gives us enough background and interest that we care for the characters; we could pine for their well-being quite easily. We see the anesthesiologist at home unhappy; we see Cherry leaving her job (we learn that her dream was to be a doctor); El Wray is a superhero *badass* reminiscent of the 1970s blaxploitation films. (Notably, in *"Planet Terror* Redux: Miscegenation and Family Apocalypse" Enrique García considers El Wray as a figure who, like his blaxploitation predecessors, draws awareness to issues of exploitation and oppression.)

AUDIENCES TODAY *AND YESTERDAY*

Rodriguez's film *Planet Terror* was purposefully constructed as a grindhouse double bill—in its conception, execution, distribution, and marketing. In addition to the umbrella title "Grindhouse" used, even before the film proper begins Rodriguez creates the trailer for *Machete* a film he had yet to make—to solidify in the audience's mind that he seeks to revitalize a prior film-going experience. The film sounds and looks like an earlier era of filmmaking. It seeks to establish a grindhouse film-viewing contract with the audience. Jay McRoy would make such an ideal audience, writing that it along with *Death Proof* "endeavor to reproduce an increasingly obsolete viewing experience for contemporary Cineplex audiences. Specifically, their ambitious collaboration aims to replicate the historically, technologically, and geographically specific 'feel' of viewing exploitation films, often in the form of damaged or incomplete prints, within a spatially and temporally specific locale, namely the derelict, often financially imperiled, urban theatres that 'flourished' in the 1960s and 1970s before slowly vanishing from the North American landscape with the emergence and proliferation of video cassettes and cable television channels" (222).

The exhibition of double and even sometimes triple bills happened mostly in inner-city theaters, or grindhouses. The theaters were quite grand at one point, but usually run-down by the 1970s. They were also screened at the more rural-set drive-ins. Because it was only one reel that would pass from city to city, they usually became quite scratched and damaged over time and with wear. Jack Stevenson describes the grindhouse theater experience:

The dialogue of the films is absolutely incomprehensible, and the easy-listening music that predominates on the soundtracks is distorted and wobbly beyond belief, like something coming from under water. They keep the projectors running *at all times* because the last thing anybody ever wants to happen is for the lights to come on. When splices break and the film suddenly stops, patrons are left to sit for long periods in total darkness. Movies start and end without any warning, logic, or continuity. (148)

And, while most critics considered grindhouse in contrast to the art-house exhibition spaces, their histories crossed. At a certain moment in history, the art house and grindhouse shared exhibition spaces. As Jack Stevenson notes, they "shared the same ghetto called 'specialty cinema.' The major producer–exhibitors denied them access to the big Hollywood star vehicles and their guaranteed grosses, forcing them to settle for crumbs" ("Grindhouse and Beyond" 129). In the 1970s, for instance, many a "failing arthouse began to book porn.[. . .] Grindhouse—porn being a form of it—had moved in to possess the corpse of arthouse, the final and most ironic disfigurement of its precious memory" (130). Stevenson continues, "To respectable citizens, inner-city porn theaters (and the grindhouses which originally served the same social function) were dens of menace, criminality, and unspeakable perversion" (131). They appeared to be spaces that existed "outside the laws and social norms of the cities in which they were located, very much in the tradition of the grindhouses" (135).

Often, the films that would be screened at the grindhouse theaters would be mostly low-budget films; many were the same film, but with a change of title. They usually were of the soft-porn sexploitation or violent exploitation kind that would pick up on any of the hot topics du jour: women in prison, motorcycle gangs, moralistic dramas, imported horror, blaxploitation films, gore trash, violent youth flicks, moonshiner shoot-'em-ups, teen-gang thrillers, sexual awakening melodramas, and lesbian vampires.

In *Grindhouse: The Sleaze-Filled Saga of an Exploitation Double Feature* (2007) Rodriguez mentions Roger Corman. Corman was known for mixing up different subgenres within one film: blaxploitation suddenly morphs into car-chase action adventure that then turns into women-in-prison flick. He also began directing at a young age, making over fifty feature films and producing over two hundred. He also worked quickly. In 1959, for instance, he made eleven films, including *A Bucket of Blood*, which was shot in five days; the quickness of his filmmaking meant that he would usually turn a profit—and, as Seth Cagin and Philip Dray write, "this permitted him to risk greater experimentation" (51). Just as theaters screened both art-house and grindhouse films, we can think of Corman's career as not so clear-cut. He gave directing opportunities to

Francis Ford Coppola, Martin Scorsese, and Jonathan Demme, among others. (See Roger Corman's insightful *How I Made a Hundred Movies in Hollywood and Never Lost a Dime*.)

Planet Terror establishes a contract at the outset. It is one where we expect it to be of the exploitation variety mostly screened at grindhouse theaters and therefore with a certain related textual experience. Once the story unfolds, we see more clearly that it is aimed at an ideal audience that doesn't mind explosions, violence, cannibalism, and scantily clad women; while there is romance, it is a film that makes few concessions to a chick-flick, say, audience. Rodriguez is clear about his ideal audience and sets himself his aesthetic goals and means to make a film for this ideal audience. This is why the film succeeds as a coherent, aesthetic whole. It is why a critic like Javier A. Martinez identifies its strength in its capacity to simultaneously occupy the genre of the "horror film about encroaching zombie hordes" and the genre of the "sf film about an experimental gas that unleashes a biological plague" (331). It is why Martinez can revel in its over-the-top comic quality as well as appreciate it as a "splatter-fest drive-in film; a fetish film; a tragic love story; a film about the creation of a Latino utopia" (331).

BEASTLY BEAUTIES

Rodriguez's *Planet Terror* functions within the aesthetic conventions of the grotesque. It combines the beautiful with the ugly to create a new perceptual, emotional, and cognitive relationship with the viewer. We see the influence of Italian horror: Dario Argento's *Four Flies on Grey Velvet* (1972), Lucio Fulci's *Zombie* (1979), and Antonio Margheriti's *Cannibal Apocalypse* (1980). The influence of George Romero's *Night of the Living Dead* (1968) is undeniable; he even casts Tom Savini—from George Romero's *Night of the Living Dead*. Here, however, Rodriguez doesn't give us traditional zombies, but rather people who become infected and then become mindless killers. He wanted to stay away from the traditional zombie look, stating, "They don't all have shriveled skin and a grayish pallor with sunken cheeks and the rotted teeth. We wanted to come up with something fresh and new. Our research took us to skin disease reference as our basis" (*Grindhouse* 101).

We could read Rodriguez's zombies as another way of portraying otherness. Annalee Newitz, drawing on a history of story from H. P. Lovecraft's Cthulhu tales to *Birth of a Nation* and *Blade*, writes: "Racial hybridity is a living death, and the desire for racial others is always tinged with fear and guilt" (*Pretend We're Dead* 91). She continues, "Slavery and genocide may be part of the past, but they wreak havoc in the present. Zombies, vampires, and mummies bear in their half-alive bodies the signs of great social injustice whose effects cannot ever be entirely extinguished" (91). Annalee Newitz identifies how extreme horror in zombie and other monster constructions that involve graphic death, mutilation, cannibalism, and the like "allegorize extremes of economic boom and bust in the United States" (*Pretend We're Dead* 12). Newitz argues that it is not only the self-made man that the capitalist machine generates as ideological fantasy, but also "gore-soaked narratives of social destruction" (*Pretend We're Dead* 15).

However, it is likely simpler than this. Rodriguez seeks to work within the zombie genre and to deform it by infusing into his film other ready-made genres like sci-fi. He seeks to make a film with a grotesque sensibility realized in a new combination of the horror with the sci-fi. Thomas Sipos identifies this hybrid genre generally as depicting monsters who come into existence by reason of rational explanation—an experiment gone awry—but who nonetheless pose an unnatural threat because "they are either newly discovered or newly created. They are unnatural to our previous understanding of the universe" (Sipos 11). For audiences to register the monsters as unnatural, a director like Rodriguez establishes a rational explanation: the exposure of the biochemical agent DC2 leads humans to mutate into zombies and cannibals. He then uses the ingredients (music, lighting, editing) that typify the horror genre to build suspense and, well, *horror*.

However, Rodriguez throws the audience a final curveball as the film comes to an end. He writes in a utopian ending: Cherry leading the people to the Promised Land we recognize as Tulum, Mexico. Rodriguez blurs all sorts of generic lines and audience expectations. He at once generates the prototypical emotion of horror—a sustaining of the emotional effect of fear—then turns this upside down with the ending. That is, he uses genres to create in the audience a new, unexpected response to the formulaic and familiar.

Rodriguez chooses horror and sci-fi genres to pave the way for the realization of his grotesque aesthetic. Stated otherwise, his ideal filmgoer will delight in his use of the aesthetic of the grotesque. The ideal filmgoer will allow himself or herself to believe that a character could transform from go-go dancer to cannibalized amputee and from disabled to machine-gun-strutting woman warrior. That is, these ideal filmgoers would allow themselves the possibility of following the film's seemingly absurd, but totally coherent logic; they would accept this transformation as possible, and not question this or anything about it such as: How does she pull the gun's trigger? How does the machine gun work also as a rocket-launcher that jettisons her over a gigantic wall? This filmgoer would then experience the simultaneous pleasure and disgust, horror and amazement, laughter and repulsion in the relishing of the aesthetics of the ugly and the beautiful as embodied in the singular entity of a character like Cherry.

Planet Terror (2007). Bruce Willis as Lieutenant Muldoon morphing into a monster.

She, like the film as a whole, is this mixture we find in the genre of the grotesque. It means that when Rodriguez builds his characters and their actions, he doesn't have to give any detailed, logical, rational explanation about these sorts of things. It means that he doesn't have to make any concessions to any everyday or religious or moral or ethical ideological doxa.

The ideal filmgoer will understand the character and film as a whole to be made with a comic-book, Tex Avery sensibility. We see plenty of action films where people launch across walls, but none where the character had her leg mauled off then a machine gun/grenade launcher attached that allows her to defeat armies of zombie invaders—and fly over walls. As such, it is an audience that would appreciate all the gadgets and weapons: from the miniature motorbike to the way the anesthesiologist wields her needles as weapons to Cherry's machine-gun leg. It's an audience that would not scream, but laugh and go *eww*! because they are repulsed and amazed when, in a Tex Avery cinematic moment, mad-scientist Abby's head explodes and splits in half, but to a comical effect. Likewise, Lieutenant Muldoon (Willis) transforms into a monstrous ball of pustules—reminiscent of Carpenter's *The Thing*. The ideal filmgoer would appreciate Rodriguez's visual and verbal gags, considering them fresh, original within the horror/sci-fi genre. Why, because he's working confidently within the genre in ways that vitally engage with the grotesque.

Rodriguez works well when he's mastered a genre. It is then that we see him exploit all its possibilities, even in its recombination with other genres. For Rodriguez, the constraints of genre, paradoxically, liberate possibilities; the clear-cut constraints and boundaries lead to a clear-cut notion of what his audience is and should be and therefore what conventions of the genre he will use directly and which he will deform through use of the aesthetic of the grotesque—directly and in subterranean, subtle ways. In a word, Rodriguez brings innovation and freshness to his films because he creates films that appreciate well his given ideal filmgoer—one who will appreciate in films (zombie, spy kids, or otherwise) his working within an aesthetic of the grotesque where anything goes.

His ideal filmgoers check their ideological baggage at the theater door. Once they are in the theater and the film unfolds, they don't criticize, for instance, the representation of Cherry as disabled or as a fetish object. Rather, they engage with her character on her terms, as does, for instance, critic Jeffrey A. Brown. He considers her "half sex-kitten, half machine gun" who "blasts away monsters and would-be rapists alike, and eventually becomes the high priestess of a post-apocalyptic new world" (101). (For a contrastive response that critiques her representation of disabled people, see Chivers and Markotic.)

POSTAPOCALYPSE *FIN*

As I mentioned already, Rodriguez chooses to depict a postapocalyptic moment as the film's concluding sequence. In the backdrop, we see the twisted remains of city buildings—not only symbolic of the decay of capitalism but also an homage to the absurdist architecture seen in Fritz Lang's expressionist film *Dr. Mabuse, The Gambler* (1922). The depiction of the twisted-up steel, skeletal frames of the existing buildings, reinforces the idea of the barbarism and the degree of destruction of civilization. Rodriguez's camera leaves this image to settle on the ragtag brigade on its journey to the beauty of the Mayan coastline—and the ruins of Tulum. It is as if Rodriguez suggests that to rebuild our civilization, we would have to rebuild it from the most advanced forms of the primitive civilizations such as the Maya.

The ending is one infused with hope. The final minutes of the film are the only sequence shot during the day, standing as a stark contrast to the entire film set at night, and that intends to lift the audience mood. Rodriguez portrays Cherry as a new millennial *Virgen de Guadalupe* who leads her postapocalyptic wandering tribe to safety. When a zombie attacks, she quickly pulls out her Gatling-gun peg leg and blasts him into oblivion. Javier Martinez remarks, this "is the new Cherry, mother to her child and to a people, whose sexuality is recast and channeled into her role as mother, protector and leader" (334). The final image of the film: Rodriguez freezes the medium-close-up shot of Cherry's face with her child (we assume to be El Wray's, and therefore mixed-race Latino/ Anglo) and imbues it with a certain painterly feel, as if it were a painting ready to go to a museum. The final frame is at once highly stylized and aesthetic, hopeful, and utopian. Christopher González considers this ending as sugges-

Planet Terror (2007). Rose McGowan as Cherry-cum–Virgin of
Guadalupe, leading her people to the promised land.

tive of a new space for the inclusion of new identities. He writes, "Rodriguez
expertly defamiliarizes the ways in which social groups can be united in the face
of terror despite differing identities" (forthcoming). For González, Rodriguez
articulates a "post post-Latinidad" that sidesteps "overt markers of Latinidad
and instead uses a handful of decisive signs of Latinidad in specific moments in
his cinematic storyworlds" (forthcoming). Likewise, Enrique García considers
the ending as the expression of a rebirth of a more inclusive American family
and nation (forthcoming).

Grindhouse has its own aesthetic as a storytelling form. It is an aesthetic
based on the exploitation of sex, race, science fiction, horror, and action in its
original forms. So what Rodriguez does is to take these ingredients and inject a
heavy dose of his aesthetics of the grotesque. In this way, he goes way beyond
the aesthetics of the grindhouse, infusing it with *newness* at the level of content
and form: a grindhouse-styled flick that brings together the primitive (zombies
and pustulating monsters) with the beautiful (Cherry and her cherubic infant)
in the realization of his aesthetics of the grotesque.

MACHETE (2010)

MACHETE BEGAN AS A TRAILER RODRIGUEZ MADE TO
establish the exploitation (and more largely, the Tex Avery/
grotesque aesthetic) contract with the viewers of *Planet Terror*. Rodriguez re-

ceived much attention for the trailer alone. Indeed, this making of a trailer before the film proper simply made visible one of Rodriguez's modes of operation: to make a trailer during the making of a film as a nutshell encapsulation of its energy, essence, and worldview as a reminder to himself. Of course, with *Machete* he does this even before making the film proper. While Rodriguez made the trailer during the summer of 2006 when he was shooting *Planet Terror*, the idea of turning Danny Trejo into the knife-wielding superhero "Machete" character had already occurred to Rodriguez while making *Desperado*; here Trejo played the knife-throwing assassin Navajas. (After the success of the trailer, he inaugurated the South by Southwest Grindhouse trailers contest. Jason Eisener's trailer, for instance, won him the attention and resources to create the exploitation-styled *Hobo With a Shotgun*.)

From the trailer, Rodriguez built his story. He calls this "reverse-engineering a movie" (Savlov). He, along with veteran Troublemaker editor Ethan Maniquis as codirector, began production of the film on July 29, 2009, and wrapped soon after on September 24. He also brought others on board, including the sharing of the script writing with Alvaro Rodriguez, DP Jimmy Lindsey (he also worked on *Sin City*), and coediting with Rebecca Rodriguez. Music from his Mexican rock band, Chingon (formed in 2003 to record songs for *Once Upon a Time*), makes up the score. Just as the trailer promises, *Machete* the film takes audiences back to a time of B-movie exploitation when anything goes, including sexagenarians who kick ass and get the scantily clad young women.

The Weinstein brothers passed on distributing *Machete*. After their investment with *Grindhouse* didn't meet expected profit margins, they considered it too much of a financial gamble. So Rodriguez gave it to Rupert Murdoch's 20th Century Fox to distribute; they were also distributing *Predators*—a Troublemaker Studios production. On September 3, 2010, *Machete* opened at 2,670 locations and 3,400 screens across the United States. Making $14 million over the Labor Day weekend, it cleared its production cost of $10.5 million. It went on to make $44 million worldwide.

While it did well commercially, it certainly hit a nerve with some critics, in terms of both its form and content. Vadim Rizov considers efforts to achieve the thrills of his "spiritual brother Quentin Tarantino" (70) a failure. He is critical of Rodriguez's lack of pacing and his use of the same locations that give it the feel of a "visibly cheap production" (70). Other critics responded to its content. Some considered *Machete* simple propaganda and a tool of the left in its opposition to Arizona's anti-immigration laws: "The film's politics are as one-sided as any Michael Moore film, casting opponents of illegal immigration as monsters to be shunned, shot or both. The film's B-movie attitude made such platitudes easier to swallow than your standard one-sided documentary, but it still cast a good chunk of the country in an unflattering light" ("Did Politics Kill 'Machete'").

Whether critical of form or content or both, these representative criticisms evince a certain failure on the part of the interpreter to step into the shoes of the ideal audience that the film itself so clearly identifies. Even before the story proper begins, the preface-like opening sequence (before the title credits appear) tells us that the film aims to entertain as a player in the Mexploitation/grindhouse tradition—and then to turn this upside down. As French critic Charlotte Garson summarizes, in other of his films he has used the low-budget exploitation/grindhouse genre approach of adopting quickly topical controversial subject matter to use as a backdrop to the film ("Mexploitation" para. 43). However, Garson also considers how *Machete* ups the ante on the exploitation/grindhouse genre, writing how it places

> le revival Grindhouse au second plan comme dans cette autre fausse bande-annonce diffusée sur Internet cet été, avec le même Machete, pour s'opposer à une nouvelle loi migratoire proposée en Arizona./ the Grindhouse revival in a secondary plane, as in this other false preview shown through the Internet this summer, with the same *Machete*, in order to oppose a new migration law proposed in Arizona. ("Mexploitation" 43; translation mine)

Zachary Ingle is another critic who manages to assess the film on its own terms. He situates the film within the blaxploitation tradition, but does so also acknowledging how it draws critical attention to how the "Latino Threat Narrative" justifies the exploitation and oppression of Latinos (forthcoming). He identifies how the film ends with undocumented émigrés fighting alongside all variety of U.S. born and raised Latinos.

At the end of the day, it's pretty difficult to reduce this to a propaganda film. There's a deliberate constructedness about it that foregrounds its playfulness and insistence that it be engaged with as an aesthetic, fictional artifact. Indeed, as Alvaro Rodriguez (credited writer on *Machete*) remarked to me, "a lot of what I brought to the project was using the simplicity and directness of the trailer ('double-crossed . . . left for dead . . .') as a shell to smuggle a sociopolitical contraband." Alvaro went on to describe *Machete* as mirroring reality, but using a "funhouse mirror in which everything is distorted but remains based on truth."

I mentioned the preface-like introduction of the film that establishes a B-flick contract with the reader; its deliberately scratched, damaged look (also seen with *Planet Terror*) asks that we place ourselves in the mind-set of

Machete (2010). Michelle Rodriguez as Shé—the superheroic leader of
Latinos.

a B-movie, celluloid aesthetic. This exaggerated texturing of the film, together
with the 1970s-style music, acts to foreground its own constructedness as fiction—and not political pamphlet or tool of propaganda. As the film unfolds,
it does refer to issues we might recognize in our everyday lives such as immigration and its laws, but it's a complete reordering of such building blocks of
reality into an aesthetic object. That is, as a film that participates within the exploitation storytelling mode, *Machete* does take up topical issues; and it does
manipulate its audience to respond to these topics. We laugh, presenting clear
signposts that the film is irreverent, parodic—the grotesque *writ large*. At the
same time, the film covers serious issues such as the dangers of crossing the
border, redneck vigilantism, corruption of politicians, and exploitation of undocumented workers.

As we see with Rodriguez's other films, yet again he attracts well-known
stars to the film. In each case, he choreographs movement, gesture, facial expression, and idiolect to convey effectively a Tex Avery, comic-book style and
worldview. Robert De Niro plays a caricature of a reactionary politician. He
plays Senator McLaughlin, who ends up, in an ironic twist of fate that could
only happen in a film like *Machete*, mistaken for an undocumented border
crosser and hunted by his own pack of redneck vigilantes. Jessica Alba plays up
her role as Sartana Rivera—the clean-cut, goodie-two-shoes Latina U.S. Im-
migrations agent. However, as the film unfolds, her moral compass shifts and
so too does her virginal sensibility give way to slinky expressions of desire for
Machete. Don Johnson exaggerates his role as the border vigilante, Von Jackson. And Michelle Rodriguez plays the tough yet sympathetic taco truck owner,
Luz. At the end, she morphs into the super-heroic leader of Latinos (undocumented and otherwise), Shé.

As Rogelio Torrez, Steven Seagal performs an exaggerated caricature of himself—of his roles in prior martial-arts films—and lays on thick a heavily accented Spanglish. Others include Jeff Fahey, who caricatures the racist, corrupt businessman, Michael Booth; Lindsay Lohan plays April, the not-so-innocent, drug-addled daughter; Cheech Marin plays the gun-toting Padre. (Notably, in Rodriguez's so-called engineering of the film in reverse, both Marin and Fahey reprise their roles from the original trailer.) Tom Savini plays the over-the-top hit man, Osiris Amanpour. Finally, Trejo plays Machete, a former Mexican *federal* who, at one point, dresses as a janitor while attempting to kill Senator McLaughlin. Again, for Rodriguez's ideal audience, the parody is clear. By dressing as a janitor, as a Latino he's even more invisible to the world. Just as the audience chuckles to this literal embrace of type, we are also meant to relish the moment when he wields a mop as weapon to combat attackers. The ideal filmgoer is likewise supposed to chuckle—and see the seriousness behind it—when he picks up a weed whacker and pickax so Booth's bodyguards will mistake him for a gardener. Again, Rodriguez plays on a mainstream sense of the Latino as gardener. Michael Booth's henchmen consider him such, even though he's wearing his trademark leather jacket. The message: no matter the outfit, a Latino carrying a weed whacker and a pickax *is a gardener*. He then subsequently uses the gardening tools to subdue, cartoon-style, the bodyguard buffoons.

The caricatures upon caricatures—caricaturing squared, if you will—set the parodic tone of the film. It wants the audience to have fun, and at the same time see with penetrating vision the commonplace treatment of and regard for Latinos. It also establishes the mood for a storyworld where the action hero who gets all the girls belies the stereotypical action hero mold. Danny Trejo's deeply

Machete (2010). *Danny Trejo as Machete "disguised" as a gardener.*

Machete (2010). Danny Trejo as Machete living it up with a mother and daughter pair, June (Alicia Rachel Marek) and April (Lindsay Lohan).

etch-marked face with hanging skin shows his age (sixty-six years old at the time) and stature (5 ft. 7 in.); he is the Latino action hero—an incorruptible Mexican *federal* who loses his family (murdered) and works as a day laborer until he can exact revenge. Rodriguez's camera and lighting embrace Trejo as the sexagenarian superhero. He even has him seemingly die (a bullet to the head) and experience a Christic resurrection of sorts (Batman and Iron Man come to mind) whereby he achieves superhuman feats, thus entering the realm of superhero mythology.

Today, we don't often see those in their sixties depicting action heroes on the silver screen. When they do appear, their old age is visually compensated for by the presence of a younger sidekick. Yet, Rodriguez chooses to populate his story with villains and a superhero that are middle-aged and elderly. In a discrete way, Rodriguez asks that his ideal audience absorb the film as part of the aesthetic of the grotesque that belongs to a predigital, less hip epoch. He's asking the ideal audience for a supplementary suspension of disbelief. This is reinforced by his use of the damaged, analogic look that he gives to the film. In a sense, too, Rodriguez is asking the audience to judge his characters and their actions in a less twenty-first-century cynical way—especially as concerns the scenes with sex. That is, he seeks to widen the audience's sphere of suspension of disbelief, transporting us to a prelapsarian age when action heroes would get the job done by brute force *and* get the girls. The romantic couplings in the film convey little romantic sentiment. They are there to convey an older Latino action hero who is sexually attractive to younger women—a characteristic quality of an earlier period of action films when this age gap was commonplace.

And yet, as already mentioned, the film is very contemporary in terms of the social and political issues that it touches on. It depicts a contemporary reality with great seriousness. It depicts the violence toward and murder of Mexicans and Central and South Americans who cross the border daily as a way to survive. It depicts the corruption and duplicity of politicians who say one thing and do the opposite. Mirroring the reality of politics and capitalism today, the characters Senator McLaughlin and businessman Michael Booth both say that they are protecting the interests of American workers and that they have a humanist approach to the treatment of undocumented Latinos, but they are actually making big profits in their exploitation. All these acute problems that come from our present-day reality are portrayed in the film.

Rodriguez, however, uses his trademark aesthetic of the grotesque to make a film in which the audience can hold in one hand both the serious and the comic-book sensibility. I already mentioned the janitor and gardener moments that express the comic-book sensibility, but there are also other moments. When Machete survives a bullet to the head, it is because that bullet hits another one already lodged there from an earlier incident. And when Luz (or "light") is shot in the eye, she reappears seemingly moments later with an eye patch ready for battle as Shé. The defiance of physical laws is the Tex Avery sensibility. It's *Droopy*. It's *Screwball Squirrel*. It is the form whereby Rodriguez can deliver the beautiful (Alba as Sartana and Rodriguez as Shé) side by side with the not so beautiful (Machete) — and all within the stylistic envelope of parody. We can have in our minds the depiction of serious problems with cartoon-like resurrections and triumphalist battles. We can have a caricature of the sexploitation B-flick (the woman who betrays Machete in the prologue-like beginning takes a cell phone out of her vagina) and the seriousness of the true-life, documentary aspect of reality: Senator McLaughlin shoots and kills a pregnant Latina crossing the border. (In 2011, the news reported how seventy Mexicans were shot dead by drug gangs, including several pregnant women.)

Like most of Rodriguez's films, there is in *Machete* the presence of the Tex Avery comic-book worldview. And, within this trademark, comic-book sensibility, there is very frequently parody. Here he chooses the Mexploitation genre as the container that holds this Tex Avery comic-book sensibility — a worldview contained within the larger aesthetic of the grotesque. As such, he asks that the ideal audience not judge the film entirely by using it as a measuring stick of reality — a measurement that would lead to the misidentification of the film as propaganda or political pamphlet. Rather, with *Machete*, Rodriguez asks his audience to mix in our minds the documentary dimension (the harsh reality of migration and exploitation of the undocumented and also the whole political and legal system that is based in the United States on favoring all forms of exploitation under capitalism) with the comic-book dimension. He wants us to at once use our brain to think politically about exploitation and the corrupt state of capitalism (to use our reality-structure functioning brain, say) and to enjoy the fantasy of this comic-book film (to use our dream-structure functioning brain, say).

If we take into account that the film also wants us to step back to an earlier epoch of existence (at least on the silver screen), then Rodriguez's full realization of the aesthetic of the grotesque in *Machete* asks the filmgoer to experience a multilayered suspension of disbelief: sexagenarian Latino action hero, the anything-goes comic-book sensibility, and a commentary on the harsh reality of immigration and exploitation faced by Latinos today.

Interestingly, and perhaps a little ironically, the infusion of the Tex Avery, anything-goes comic-book sensibility in the film *Machete* is not at all present in Rodriguez's comic book. Indeed, Rodriguez's and Aaron Kaufman's (writers) along with Stuart Sayger's (artist) comic book *Machete* #0 (2010), published in near simultaneity with the film's release, follows much more directly the "documentary" ingredient mentioned above. That is, while Rodriguez chooses the comic-book format to tell this story (a prequel to the film) he does so to subordinate completely the Tex Avery worldview and instead emphasize the hard-hitting "realism" of the violence directed at women on the Mexican side of the U.S./Mexico border. This is to say, the characterization of Machete in the comic book is straight-faced vigilantism. There are no layers of parody, satire, or the anything-goes sensibility that we see in the film. In this dark world (inked with grays, yellows, and black) Daniel "Machete" Lopez takes matters into his own hands when he realizes that the authorities don't care about the women's murders, including the bloody slaying of a Latina from the nearby town, Nezahualcóyotl. At the scene of the murder one *federal* tells another, "Who really gives a shit about one more mujer anónima?" An angry Machete appears in the panel that follows: "*I* give a shit!" As he sleuths out the murderer he encounters male teenagers from Nezahualcóyotl who reflect this sense of Latinas as disposable objects: "Hey, man, girls go missing all the time. It just . . . happens. If you young and even close to pretty in this town, you in danger." And another remarks, "*Nobody cares*. Look at us—we live in garbage, old man. Ain't no cops coming around to police *this* neighborhood."

In the comic-book world, Rodriguez chooses to leave the "comic-book" sensibility aside. Instead, he deftly uses a varied palette of geometric shapes of bodies and objects as well as panel sizes along with strategically placed verbal elements (balloons as well as voice-over-narrator boxes) to convey a straight-up social-realist story. Machete finds the murderer, and after slicing his head in half, he states: "I tried to do the right thing. But they pissed off the wrong Mexican this time!" This is a world where violence against women is the norm. This is a world with no hope. It is a world filled with corruption and where the nation-state fails its citizens — especially the most vulnerable members, women and children. It is a world where there is no future for the new generation who are numbed to violence and atrocity.

MACHETE KILLS (2013)

ONCE AGAIN, RODRIGUEZ BRINGS HIS COMIC-BOOK, Tex Avery worldview to *Machete Kills*. However, while in *Machete* he uses this anything-goes approach as the envelope that contains both the playful (from Machete's janitorial combat moves to Shé's resurrection) and serious (from the deadly border crossing to murderous minutemen and senators), in *Machete Kills* the playful dominates.

Distributed by Open Road (or ORF), the $20-million–budgeted *Machete Kills* opened on October 11, 2013, in 2,538 theaters across the United States. Opening against much larger budget films such as Alfonso Cuarón's *Gravity*, Paul Greengrass's *Captain Phillips*, and John Francis Daley's *Cloudy with a Chance of Meatballs 2*, *Machete Kills* ranked No. 4 — pulling in $3.8 million at the box office by the end of the weekend.

As with *Machete*, Rodriguez uses the first five minutes as a prologue of sorts to establish the contract with his viewers. The action takes place at a cement factory on the Arizona/Mexico border where ex-*migra* agent Sartana Rivera (Jessica Alba) and Machete Cortez (Danny Trejo) mow down several dozen mercenary soldiers: blood spurts and gushes as appendages are sliced and bodies are bisected. Before Rivera is shot dead by a luchador-masked villain, she reminds Machete (and the audience), "You taught me that the law and justice are not always the same thing." The last we had seen of this dynamic duo was their riding not off into the sunset (as per its Western generic conceit), but Rivera straddling Machete as they travel down the road on his motorbike. It was playfully romantic but with the message left loud and clear: they have both decided to follow the life of outlawed *justicieros* with their sole purpose in life being to fight for justice in a world filled with corrupt politicians and billionaires who use the law to exploit the disenfranchised. While Rivera reminds Machete of this dichotomy of justice and law in *Machete Kills*, as the story proper begins and unfolds this concept and the *real* fight for *real* justice is increasingly left behind. There is fighting — lots of it — but nearly exclusively tied to a tired save-the-world conceit that turns *Machete*'s fight for actual justice into a largely empty abstraction.

Unmoored from the gravitas of everyday material concerns, *Machete Kills* uses the intertextual sight gag (typically by allusion to Rodriguez's own cinematic oeuvres and to genre films generally) as the generator of plot and character trait. The film introduces U.S. President Rathcock (played by Charlie Sheen, identified by his birth name, Carlos Estévez) as a cursing, smoking, gun-toting lover of many women. He identifies Machete as the best man for the job (to apprehend the revolutionary, Marcus Mendez, played by Demián Bichir), declaring him to not only know Mexico the best but to be "Mexico." If Machete accepts the mission to save the United States (and then the world), Rathcock offers him legal residency. When we meet Madame Desdemona (played by Sofía Vergara, and an allusion to the many dominatrices that populate the Bond world such as Fatima Bush and Pussy Galore), she asks for her ironclad "double D" bra and then her "strap-on" that all fire rounds of bullets. In a final duel between Shé (Michelle Rodriguez) and the double-crossing, bilingual Miss San Antonio (played by actress Amber Heard, who came out in 2013 as bisexual in an interview for *Elle* magazine), she's fighting blind: one patch over an eye shot in *Machete* and the other shot out in *Machete Kills*. The traces of blood dripping from her eye socket allude directly to the same bloodied, hollowed eye socket look of Sheldon Jeffrey Sands (played by Johnny Depp) in the final showdown in *Once Upon a Time in Mexico*.

The allusions (or Easter eggs) to other of Rodriguez's films like *Planet Terror* run deep and wide. And, so, too, do the allusions to other films like Lewis Gilbert's 1979 *Moonraker* (Marko Zaror plays a Latino-fied bodyguard akin to Jaws, and Mel Gibson, as Luther Voz, a Hugo Drax), Lucas's 1977 *Star Wars* (a landspeeder appears), and Kubrick's 1964 *Dr. Strangelove* (Machete rides a nuclear bomb much like Major T. J. "King" Kong), which begin to pile up— much like the body count.

It's not that *Machete* wasn't packed with caricatures, but with them there was also an interesting and intellectually challenging backdrop: it dealt with the very serious problem of the murdering of people trying to cross the border or who have already made it across the border from Central America and Mexico but are still hunted as wildlife or as dehumanized "aliens." It also dealt with the exploitation of immigrants without a visa in American fields and factories. In a clear and serious way, *Machete* did show the deep separation (a chasm, actually) between justice and law. In terms of justice, all workers on U.S. soil, both national and immigrants, should have the same rights and should not be exploited, for they are all part and parcel of the same social and economic class. This outlook functions as a thematic background in the whole of *Machete*, but it is no longer present in *Machete Kills*, where the motive becomes as outlandishly abstract as its continuous explosions and fights and (sometimes private) jokes and allusions and intertextuality, all of which end up being superficial, imitative, and not at all creative. In short, in *Machete* there is present a central story thread that keeps the audience's brain busy and that is submitted to a cartoon treatment that is aesthetically enjoyable.

In contrast, in *Machete Kills* we have a cartoon with an abundance of intertextual allusions that exist without any apparent purpose. It's as if the film's generator were its visual jokes and *intertextuality*, and not its story or subject matter. We as audience may recognize the intertextual allusions to other films by both Rodriguez and other directors and filmic genres, and perhaps smile or chuckle as they appear, but this does not lead to an aesthetic gratification, for the cartoon approach pervades everything — images and story — and is paramount. It's just there, making no contribution to anything we see on the screen. It appears gratuitous, misguided, and certainly insufficiently thought through.

This lack of command over the film as a whole is perhaps rooted in the lack of a clear vision on what the story should be telling us and therefore on who it is addressing. *Machete Kills* illustrates once again the perils of not identifying correctly the purported audience. The conceit, as such, therefore implodes — like one of the imploding sci-fi-fashioned guns used in the film — and there's nothing really left to appreciate and remember it by. The upshot is that *Machete Kills* conveys the overwhelming sense of an incoherent whole, or blueprint, that wanders wherever the mind wanders: from *justiciero* narrative to sci-fi film palimpsest to Tex Avery cartoon.

We sense that Rodriguez (and his cowriter Marcel Rodriguez along with screenplay writer Kyle Ward) didn't ask these questions: Who are we making this film for? Who is our ideal audience? Throughout his career Rodriguez has been spot-on, making films for kids and for adults — and for different kinds of kids and adults. This is certainly less the case with *Machete Kills*.

It's a Wrap

S INCE THE MAKING OF *EL MARIACHI*, IN 1992, ROBERT
Rodriguez has created seventeen films, not including the recent
animation reboot, *Fire and Ice* or *Sin City: A Dame to Kill For* that were in different stages of production during the writing of this book. In each and together
we see proof of the fact that form and matter *are one*. They can't be separated
except in pedagogical or expository reason. They are one. We see how in the creating of his films, Rodriguez has an idea and then a form in mind, and he adapts
his matter to this form. We see how he gives shape to his thoughts, images, and
feelings through the form he has chosen. In the end we have a film (and series
of films), and if we separate form from content, we have the same effect as with
the table that has been mutilated and has only three legs: null. Rodriguez's film
career thus far is living proof of the fact that form and content, shape and matter, are inseparable. This is the organic whole and speaks directly to the fact of
the impossibility of separating the form from content without destroying the
object.

In each of Rodriguez's films, we see different expressions of what I have been
calling the overarching aesthetic of the grotesque: the melding of the attractive
with the unappealing. This is often infused, also, with a Tex Avery comic-book
sensibility. In this way, too, the shape he gives to his movies reminds the audience that his filmic narratives are in no way a copy of reality, a testimony, or a
simple statement of the fact and event. They are always creations. That is, they
are always created organic wholes. The proof of the fact that they are organic
wholes and that they are creations is that they always necessarily imply a deliberate selection of features that will constitute their content, their form, and
their substance.

They remind the filmgoer and interpreter of his films that in the making of
his aesthetic products there is deliberate selection of *what* is told and *how* this is

told. This selection implies on the part of Rodriguez the wish to obtain certain effects on the viewer. Therefore this selection also implies a choice of gaps to be filled by the audience. The filling in of these gaps requires the use of signposts to help guide the audience that are discovered in the careful study of his films.

The organic whole that constitutes each of his films is formed by that which is explicitly represented by Rodriguez in the film and all that has been left for the viewer to discover—to know without having to be directly told. In most cases, Rodriguez's films are the sum of these ingredients—ingredients of presence and absence, that which is explicitly present and that which is absent and left to the viewer to derive by logic or any other deductive process. It is this sum of the present and absent ingredients that are intended by Rodriguez to have an emotional and intellectual impact on the viewer and that therefore require the viewer to also be an active, deliberate interpreter of the film.

I've said this before and I'll say it again: Robert Rodriguez is the most prolific Latino film director of the twenty-first century. He might even be the most prolific film director of his generation worldwide. In most of his films we see that he puts his filmmaking method, approach, and goals (his *cinematic poetics*, if you will) to excellent use and with great success. According to the unified aesthetics that I formulated at the beginning of this book and paraphrased just now, when Rodriguez succeeds in his filmmaking he creates a series of unified wholes that succeed not as measured by ticket sales, but in the way he uses his filmmaking skill and imagination to create a coherence of form and content that move audiences to sense, think, and feel the world anew.

In many ways, his short films made in high school such as "Halloween IV" and "Miami Priest" and then in college with "Bedhead" present the keys to unlocking his cinematic poetics—poetics understood in terms of his general approach to his filmmaking, not a theory of filmmaking in general, but his own particular approach to making films. We see in these early shorts and especially in "Bedhead" how Rodriguez infuses his films with a comic-book sensibility—a worldview enveloped within a larger grotesque aesthetic mode. It is an invented world where anything goes, including the dragging of a brother at ninety miles an hour behind a bike. It is a world where the beautiful and the not so beautiful conjoin. It is an invented world where objects and actions function as vehicles for new ways to see, feel, and think about the world. Finally, in these early short films and all the films he has made since, Rodriguez upholds the principle that filmmaking and its consumption should be something that opens our senses, thoughts, and feelings to something new—and in an absolutely pleasurable way.

Interview with Robert Rodriguez

*T*HIS INTERVIEW TOOK PLACE AT TROUBLEMAKER Studios in Austin, Texas, on October 26, 2012. In the middle of a whirlwind of activity with the beginning of the shoot for *Sin City 2*, Robert Rodriguez took pause to sit for this interview. The interview took place in his Southwest-styled, baroque-painted office with significant props from his different movies, including the *Predators* mask hanging from one of the walls. We sat across from one another at his desk — the bar used in *Desperado*, I believe. After the interview I was invited to shadow Rodriguez for a spell. I was then invited

Frederick Luis Aldama with Robert Rodriguez at Troublemaker Studios.

by Glenda Delgado to see where the CGI/animatrics editing takes place along with the 3-D copier used to make synthetic props; the costuming and wood and metal workshop; the green screen stage (one of the old airport hangars); and the lot filled with large props such as Humvees, beefed-up cars, a helicopter, and a section of an airplane.

FREDERICK LUIS ALDAMA: I thought to begin the interview by asking questions about your very early introduction to film and filmmaking. As a kid, the VHS technology and format allowed you to get your hands on movies such as *Escape from New York*—a film that seemed to have had a big influence on you and your work. Can you talk about this film and others during the VHS moment in your early film education?

ROBERT RODRIGUEZ: I would mainly watch movies that had just come out on video. It was very new, so I would grab my favorites, like *Empire Strikes Back*, *Jaws*, and other popular blockbusters. I was drawn to fantasy, science fiction, and action films. They were entertaining. These directors and others showed me that it could be possible to make films in these genres. John Carpenter's *Escape from New York* and Sam Raimi movies made up new worlds with their own rules. *Escape from New York* just blew me away. That you could just turn New York into a prison, say that it's 1997, and have any character you want? I loved the freedom of this. Then I discovered that Carpenter did the music as well as writing and directing of the movie. I had so many interests as a kid like music, drawing, and photography that this really appealed to me. When I saw somebody like Carpenter do it all, I thought, if I went into movies, I could do all my favorite hobbies under the umbrella of one project. I didn't want to give any of my interests up. I'm still like that. I still do all these different jobs because I enjoy the creativity in each area. The technical part of each job is a little different, but the creative part is the same, no matter what job you're doing. How you apply your creativity is similar. Each area can inspire creativity in the other. So if you get stuck in one area, you skip over to the other interest. You can make a lot of creative headway doing that. Seeing the potential to create in so many different areas in movies like Carpenter's *Escape from New York* was inspirational to me.

FLA: Speaking of creativity, I've noticed in all of your movies, some more than others, an anything-can-happen vision. It's what I identify in the book as your comic-book sensibility that you bring to your films . . .

RR: People say, "You make such different movies. You make action movies, and horror movies, and kids' movies." I say, "Well, they're all the same. They're all fantasies." I've never made a realistic film. In my films anything can actually happen. I showed my trailer to *Grindhouse* to Jim Cameron. After he saw the girl, the machine-gun leg, and all the other stuff, he just went, "Wow! That's unbridled moviemaking from the id. It makes sense the moment you're watching it and not a minute afterwards." It's like my movies are all fever dreams. You wake up from a dream, and you try to tell your spouse this crazy dream you had that had you really tense, but it sounds ridiculous when retelling it. But in the moment it made total sense. That's what my movies are. They're like dream imagery — things that are not real.

My movies have a comic-book sensibility because I used to be a cartoonist. Even the more violent movies are comical. I structure the films with a timing that's like a joke setup: a one–two–three punch. They are about gags, staging, and making the audience believe something that's completely unbelievable. In the moment of watching them, you're actually buying the fact that the laws of physics and other rules all just wash away. I remember an actor once asking me, "Should I care if that shot fired six or seven times, because this is a revolver?" I responded, "They're still trying to figure out how she's shooting the machine gun leg, so don't worry about it. It's not that kind of movie at all."

FLA: Where does this impulse to have absolute freedom to create in your films come from?

RR: I have always been a person who felt restricted by rules, containment, and structure, and so the abandonment that you could have in a movie is what I found the most freeing. At the end of *Once Upon a Time in Mexico* Salma [Hayek] asks Antonio [Banderas], "What do you want?" After he says "Freedom" and she responds "So simple" he adds, "No." That's all I've ever sought is freedom — creative and professional freedom to be able to do what I want. It's why I have my own studio.

I think I got this from my dad, who was a salesman who worked for himself; all my brothers are in sales or some kind of entrepreneurial job, so they could also work for themselves. I wanted to be the boss of my own world, so I could create my own rule system.

When I was in Hollywood working on *Zorro*, one of the producers came in and saw that I had my little son in the crib at my office, and remarked to one of the other producers, "You shouldn't be bringing your kids to work." At that moment, I knew that the studio I would create would be for everybody, including those who wanted to bring their kids to work. That's how Coppola works. That's how I want to work. I don't want to be without my family. That's not how I make my movies. I didn't want to be in a system where there's a set of rules and a way that you have to be. I want to design my life in a way where movies are just a part of my life, not a job I have to go to. That's why when you come into my office it looks like my home. It's like I'm in my bedroom when I'm even at the office. This is why I have worked out of the house for so long, and still do. I don't want to feel like I have to get up and go to a *job*.

The way I see my filmmaking I can say that I've never worked a day in my life. I love the fact that what I make for my living is what I do at home anyway. I'm always creating stuff with the kids, making movies and drawing.

FLA: Is *Sharkboy and Lavagirl* a product of this play?

RR: *Sharkboy and Lavagirl* was our playtime — but with a purpose. The boss liked my son Racer's idea. I pitched Weinstein the movie, and said, "My son came up with that." He told me, "Go make that movie. We need another family film that's in 3-D." So we could sit and draw these ideas as we usually did during our drawing time, but knowing all along that this was work for a film project. It was work, but at the same time it didn't feel like work.

That's how my life is. It never feels like I'm working. I'm always having family time as creative time. At its best, making films is work time that feels like playtime. Then you always are happy.

People are surprised that I can make so many movies in such a small amount of time. People ask, "When are you going to take a break? You work so much." But to me I'm not working. They should change that word to "play" and ask the question again: "When are you going to take a break? You play too much." I don't go on vacation because I'm always on vacation. This is how I've designed my work life and my studio.

This sense of play and joy in everything is reflected in the movies. Even if it's a horror movie, there's going to be joy, and it's going to be silly, and there's going to be a lot of fun to be had. It's just how I am. I'm not a brooding guy. I don't think I could make a straight drama. I don't mind watching them, but to make them would be like robbing yourself of so much creation in moviemaking where you can invent, design, and construct everything about a shot, a set, a moment, and a prop.

There are so many invented props in my movies. In the making of *Sin City 2* we're bringing back one of the weapons I invented in *From Dusk till Dawn*: the automatic crossbow that uses a shotgun cocking system. Ch-ch and it's loaded again. This weapon doesn't exist in real life. It's just in that movie. We needed it for *Sin City 2*, so we went and dug it up in my archives. It was in a little wooden coffin. I save all those invented weapons, toys, and other props. In filmmaking, you can have the freedom to invent . . . to do anything.

FLA: How might this freedom in filmmaking express itself in the choices you make as a Latino film director?

RR: This question of identity is one of the things I'm exploring with my television network [El Rey]. The fact is, when you go to write something, you're writing it as your own person. You write what you know. So even though you're not intending to write a Latin character, because it will probably be based on yourself or your family or someone you know, most of the time, if not all of the time, it's probably going to be a Latin character. So you're going to have to cast somebody Latin.

The problem I had when I went to Hollywood was that there were no Latins working in Hollywood. It's a very reactive business. It's not really innovative. Someone has to be the first. So I had to go through *Desperado* and *Dusk till Dawn* to create my own Latin star system. The closest actor we had to a Latin star was Antonio [Banderas] so we brought him from Spain; the studios sort of knew him because of his roles in the Almodóvar movies. To break Salma into Hollywood, I had to make an entire movie, *Roadracers*. This way when I went to make *Dusk till Dawn* and the *Spy Kids* movies, she would be recognizable. When I wrote my script, which, again, just happened to be a Latin because I was Latin, I wouldn't have trouble casting her. This eventually changed the industry. It took some time, but eventually, by casting Latins over and over again, by the time I did *Sin City*, it was very easy to have Benicio del Toro, Rosario Dawson, Jessica Alba, and Alexis Bledel play all sorts of characters.

The key: if someone is trying to make a film and they're Latin, make it mainstream and accessible so it's not pigeonholed as Latin. You don't think of *Desperado* or *Dusk till Dawn* or *Machete* or *Spy Kids* as these Latin films. They are Latin films, and they're not. You have to be very clever about it. Latins don't want to feel like they have to go off to a corner and watch their own movie in their own cinema. It has to be more subversive than that. You have to be very clever about it. Latin audiences want to feel like they're part of the whole world culture. That's what I mean by making sure it is mainstream and accessible.

Spy Kids has a mainstream, McDonald's tie-in. Yet, if you were Latin and you really looked at it closely, you would go, "Wow, they're Latin." The studio asked, "Why are you making them Latin? We don't understand. You're making the movies in English. Why are they Latin? We've never seen that before." I responded, "Well, it's going to be in English and it's going to be for everybody. You don't have to be British to watch James Bond, but making him British does give him a more specific identity, which makes him more universal." I won with this argument.

It's a very reactive business. This just shows that we not only need to pressure Hollywood to write more Latin characters, but we need more Latin filmmakers who can go in and make that argument and create in their own image so that it's authentic, and yet universal.

FLA: I like the way you talk about creating characters with specific identities as a way for them to have a universal appeal to all kinds of audiences. Your films are all so different. Who is your ideal audience?

RR: I'm probably that audience. I try to please myself first. My movies have a very distinct point of view. If you don't care for the movie, well, then that's fine, but at least you can say it's got a point of view. On the other hand, there are movies that feel as if too many people were involved. You might ask, "Whose movie is it, and what's the point of view?" At this point, the movie is not true to anybody. Take it or leave it—I try to make the best possible movies that are true to somebody. I can sleep well at night knowing that I did everything I could to pull this off.

FLA: I imagine there are situations with certain pressures (producers and so on) that can make it difficult to make films with your distinctive point of view?

RR: When you're making a movie in a situation with lots of constraints and where you have to make a lot of compromises and then the result isn't welcome, then you wish more than ever that you'd given yourself your own day in court to see if your idea would have flown. I'm very satisfied with what I've done, with what I've been able to do with the means that I've had at hand. I always want to learn, and always try and get better.

FLA: At one point in *Rebel Without a Crew* you mention how every director has one bad movie in them . . .

RR: I don't remember why I said that, but I would probably say it differently now. I have made movies that succeed and fail at the box office. With those that failed, people have asked, "What do you do when you wasted a year and a half of your life on something and it failed?" And I reply, "Well, that's a real negative way to look at it. I don't look at things like that at all." I don't. I just keep making movies because you don't know which one's going to hit. I mean how can you say a movie failed? Did it really fail? My *Four Rooms* movie, "The Misbehavers," is probably my favorite short film that I've made; it's also very well received. But in the context of the movie [made up of four short films], it doesn't work as a whole. The movie itself didn't succeed financially. That doesn't mean that it was a bad idea to make the movie. In fact, it's probably the most important step I could have taken.

It's not bad to have a bad movie in you; to have a movie that doesn't succeed. Getting that bad movie out takes you to the next step. If you were to look at Jim Cameron's films, you might say, "This is probably the one that didn't perform as well," and yet that's the most important one in his whole career, that it was the seed for *Avatar*, for *Titanic*, for everything that came after.

When Quentin [Tarantino] asked me if I wanted to be part of this anthology [*Four Rooms*], my hand just went up, and I went, "Yeah." Now, should I have not followed my instinct and instead study a little bit to see that anthologies never work and in that they always bomb? No. I went ahead and made a movie that I was really fond of, but that didn't succeed. I don't look back and think this is a bad movie or that it was a failure. I look back and say, "God, when I was on the set of that, that's where I came up with the idea for *Spy Kids*"—seeing the parents that are an international couple, dressed in tuxedos, and the kids were in tuxedos 'cause it's New Year's Eve. I thought, "That's the angle I've been looking for my family film." What if these parents got kidnapped and these two kids who can barely tie their shoes have to go save them? And the movie will be called "Spy Kids"? That was in 1994. I made *Spy Kids* six years later, but I wrote it over that period.

So the anthology [*Four Rooms*] didn't really work, but I always believed in short films, and I thought an anthology could work if it was one director, not four directors, and three stories and not four, because three have structure. It's more like storytelling. And I tried it again. Why would I try another anthology, knowing that one failed? Because I thought I could figure out a way to do it right. And we did it on *Sin City*. So *Sin City* and *Spy Kids* came from *Four Rooms*.

So, I wouldn't say you have a bad movie. I would say don't fear failure. Winston Churchill says, "Success is moving from one failure to the next with great enthusiasm." By cracking some eggs, you can make some omelets. Sometimes it's not pretty, but you know that you're doing it for a reason. If you follow your instinct to go a certain way, if it doesn't work out, you know that you were there for a reason. What can you learn from that? It'll probably take you somewhere beyond where you thought you could go. I've seen this my whole career. I thought I failed in making *El Mariachi*. I made it to sell to the Spanish home-video market and it didn't. In this sense, it failed. But in another more important way, it did work out. It got bought by Columbia and went a whole other direction that I never would have imagined. So my initial plan was a failure, but the ultimate success of it was much greater than what I could have seen at the time.

FLA: Projects come across your desk. How do you decide what to make? Do you have a checklist?

RR: It's really just a timing thing for me. I have a lot of projects. I don't really get offered a lot because I tend to turn a lot of stuff down.

Early on in my career, around the time of *Dusk till Dawn*, I started getting scripts for what became *Superman Returns*, *X-Men*, *Wild, Wild West*. They were great titles, but the scripts needed a lot of work. They weren't ready to shoot at all. I would have had to go and work with writers and go through a whole process to make them workable. I thought, do I really want to put in that much work into something that I don't own and control? George Lucas wanted to make *Flash Gordon*. He couldn't get the rights, so he wrote *Star Wars*. This has always been my approach. If the script is called *X-Men* and it's ready to go, and it's perfect, and I can jump right in and make it, OK, that's very compelling. That's never the case. It usually needs so much work that you figure, let me put that work into something that I own and control, that I can say is mine, and that I can build up in my own franchises like *Spy Kids* and the *Machete* series. Now I'm working on a *Machete* trilogy, but it's very unusual for a writer–director to create several franchises — and that have a very strong Latin sensibility to them. Usually other writers or creators are involved.

I take a lot of pride in the fact that I've been able to make original material that has struck a chord with people, that I have made here in my own little incubator, in this day and age when original properties are few and far between and most things are remakes. This comes about because I turn down some of the other projects. At the end of the day I felt like I wanted the freedom to do my own thing.

I almost did *Zorro*. The highlight: I worked with Spielberg a little. He was soon off to another movie (he produces in a way where he lets you make your movie yourself), and I was left with the producers on the movie and the studios: Tri-Star still had the rights to it, and it was Amblin Entertainment's last movie. These two studios didn't get along, and I was pulled in between them. They didn't want to let me just make the decisions. They got involved so much that it felt like I was working. I felt like I was showing up and trying to please people that were not happy with each other. So I left that movie to go make *Spy Kids*. I mentioned already how my brothers and my dad are the same way. They would rather not work for somebody and be told what to do. They'd rather have their own business and make less money but be happy. That's just no fun.

FLA: If you compare the number of people mentioned in the credits at the end of *Desperado* with those at the end of *Spy Kids* it seems that the crew that makes up your "incubator" has grown. Yet you still manage to maintain that unique Rodriguez vision and point of view in your films . . .

RR: A lot of it is that I changed how things were done. I take on those jobs that are very important. Usually on a movie the size of *Sin City* or on any of the *Spy Kids* series, you always have at least one visual effects supervisor, somebody there to figure out how the shots are done, to go between the director and the vendors, to bring you the shots as they've been worked on, develop the shots, and then bring them in for approval. I fired that person a long time ago.

In making *From Dusk till Dawn* I had one visual effects supervisor. I realized then that I needed to do this important job. This way, instead of going through somebody, I could deal directly with the artists. Back when I was making *Spy Kids*, I had this thing called a sync system, where an artist team in Canada could see what I was working on. I could draw on it and they could see what I was drawing. I would say, "Change this, change that, put this there, put that there. Actually, let me edit the shot you just gave me. You know what? If you speed up frames 20 to 60 by 200 percent, the shot will work the way it is. You don't have to do any more, and I can use that. Just change this and that." By eliminating that job where somebody else shuttles stuff back and forth that wastes time and creates the possibility for miscommunication, I saved three weeks of effort by working directly with the artists.

Much of what the industry has created is a system where there are so many barriers to the creative process. It's a system that makes filmmaking difficult and cumbersome. I simplified the process so much down here [Troublemaker Studios in Austin] that I'm able to keep that direction on everything, and keep that continuity. I do my own editing. I supervise and come up with how we're going to do the shots. I invent how we're going to do all these things. I'm the director of photography. I'm involved in a lot of the production design. I write the script. And, if I haven't conveyed all the ideas and thoughts, I can compose the music — that soundtrack in your ear that tells you what to feel and think. These are the main, important jobs involved in keeping that continuity. Underneath this, you can add more armies to your crew to help get it done, but they are all being guided — every one of them.

FLA: Budget, technology, and other aspects of filmmaking might make it difficult to bring to the screen ideas, characters, and settings that you have in your mind. Have you encountered any limits to what you can do with film?

RR: I don't think there are limits to what you can do, especially with computer technology. Years back when I was first doing the *Spy Kids* movies I was able to create the Thumb Thumbs — imaginary figures that I drew when I was thirteen and that I won an art contest for. When you are able to realize your childhood dream, then anything is possible.

Now that we can do anything, what is it we're going to do? Now that anything can be done, where are we going to focus our attention? It has to come down always to the storytelling and the creating of a character that resonates with people. That's why you can go back and do something really low budget like *Machete*. It's not so much a movie about the effects as it is about a character that people latch onto and enjoy. So it comes back down to the storytelling.

As far as the limitations of budget and technology, it really is a matter of how much time and money you have. Sometimes you can only get it to look so good. You know that if you had more money and time you could make it look much better, but sometimes you just have to live with it. There are limitations. I haven't always gotten what I wanted. I've gotten sometimes a fourth of that. But if it still works, then that's fine.

When I did *Sin City*, I thought that's the best kind of movie I could do on a budget, because I'm just trying to be true to the book. The book has very little going on in the background, so I could shoot it all on green screen and if I ran out of money, all I would have to do is put black behind them and it would still be true to the source material. So even though it's not the blown-out background I would want, if I can't afford that, at the end of the day I'm still accomplishing my goal: to be true to the comic book. Anything beyond that is gravy.

If I can get the most out of an effect or an idea, then that's great. But I've budgeted it in my mind to know that at the end of the day, the idea itself has to be clever enough that even if it doesn't look great, it still works. I know that its primary purpose is not to just look amazing, but to be clever and entertaining.

FLA: At different stages of your filmmaking career you actually learned a new skill *in the actual making* of the movie: the Steadicam in *Desperado* and 3-D cameras in *Spy Kids* 3. You innovate and overcome problems by learning new technologies to find solutions. Has this also helped develop the technology itself for filmmaking?

RR: Very early on when we started using the digital cameras, we got the Sony cameras, and we shot slow motion with them by shooting 60 frames, and then turning each frame into a full frame. Sony didn't even know it could shoot slow motion. Well, it's a post–slow motion, but it works pretty well. By figuring out how to do something innovative, you push the technology. In a way, you're the one field-testing the stuff, then they would ask what you want on the next cameras and we would tell them what to modify.

By being an early adopter, you're very much on the cutting edge of technology, and people want your feedback. You're the one out in the field using it, and you can really help them make their product better. A lot of the stuff we're inventing at the time — figuring it out as we go. When we opened up the boxes and pulled out those first digital cameras, we'd call around and ask if anybody knew how to use them. Nobody had been using them, so we thought, well, we can't do anything wrong, because there's no one right way to do it. We had to figure this out, so we learned as we went along. It was very exciting to be on that cutting edge.

FLA: Looking to the future, you're in postproduction on *Machete Kills*, about to start shooting *Sin City 2*, and you have the cable channel just around the corner. Would you like to say anything about either of these projects or any others in the future?

RR: We're getting into some animation, which we haven't done before. We've been doing a lot of animation in our movies, but just characters. We haven't done a full-blown animated film. So we're trying to make some innovations there as far as how quickly we can turn something around. So that's exciting. We had a great project to work on to try this out. Since it's animated, I can do this concurrently with the other projects.

The El Rey Network is exciting. It will bring some of these low-budget techniques to television here in Austin. Having a television network will allow me to green-light the making of shows that I've always wanted to see. That will be a playground and a half. And it's a direct pipeline into people's homes, so that's pretty amazing to have that kind of distribution. It's a very rare deal. It's one of those once-in-a-lifetime opportunities, where a government requires somebody to give up a network, and I got to go in and get it and make it. So that's going to be pretty amazing. It's something that wouldn't have existed otherwise.

FLA: Finally, how do you see yourself as a director of films within the big picture of world cinema?

RR: I think the movies I've made and the work I've done have been able to inspire people. The biggest comment I get is people saying, "We love your movies, and we love your book." You can tell it inspires them to want to go do the same thing. That is the best. John Carpenter, Spike Lee, and Sam Raimi inspired me to become a filmmaker not just because of the entertainment value of their movies — they are fun — but something even bigger. They made me feel like I could go and make movies too. They hold a special place with me. It's almost as if I owe my whole career to them because they made me realize I could do this.

To help others I might inspire, I try to put as much information as possible on my DVDs about filmmaking. This way, whether you like the film or not, you can learn how it works and see how you can apply some of these techniques to your own creativity — and not necessarily just to moviemaking. It can be to anything.

I love to teach. I love to instruct people and give them insight into things that I discover. I always give away all my tricks because I would have appreciated this as a filmmaker who felt like he couldn't get into the business because he lived in Texas. I try to share anything that I think would give them some insight into how to do things. I think what people like about my movies is the idea that you're making all this happen in any way you can. This can be inspiring to other people. They can tell by the kind of actors that come work with me that they, too, are all inspired by the goodwill flowing here.

More than just the movies themselves, which are hopefully entertaining in some way, there is a goodwill that goes along with them. This is unique and special. If I wanted to run a restaurant, I'd want it to be like the ones I love, those mom-and-pop ones where you go and there's the guy behind the counter who is also the owner. His face is on the taco store, his wife's there at the counter too, and his kids are working the tables. Those are my favorite kind of restaurants. My movie business is like a family-run restaurant in that we all contribute and work together to make innovative, inspiring movies that audiences can't get at the big chains . . .

Filmography

I list several members of the principal cast. With the exception of "Black Mamba," advertisement shorts are not listed. With the exception of *Predators*, films Rodriguez produced are not listed. Feature films are dated according to year of U.S. domestic theatrical release.

"Halloween IV" (1985)
Production: Video Slugs
Direction: Robert Rodriguez
Writers: Robert Rodriguez and David O'Malley
Cinematography: Robert Rodriguez
Editing: Robert Rodriguez
Cast: John J. Garcia, Chris Orthmann, Thomas Moreno, David O'Malley, Randy Notzon
9 min.

"Miami Priest" (1986)
Production: Video Slugs
Direction: Robert Rodriguez
Writer: Robert Rodriguez
Cinematography: Robert Rodriguez
Editing: Robert Rodriguez
Cast: James Archuleta, Chris Orthmann, Thomas Moreno, Matthew Marr, Mike
    Cardenas
27 min.

"Bedhead" (1991)
Production: Sharon Courtney
Direction: Robert Rodriguez
Writer: Robert Rodriguez
Cinematography: Robert Rodriguez

Editing: Robert Rodriguez
Cast: Rebecca Rodriguez, David Rodriguez, Tina Rodriguez
Color
8 min.

El Mariachi (1992)
Production: Elizabeth Avellán, Carmen M. De Gallardo, Carlos Gallardo, Robert
   Rodriguez
Direction: Robert Rodriguez
Writer: Robert Rodriguez
Cinematography: Robert Rodriguez
Editing: Robert Rodriguez
Cast: Carlos Gallardo, Consuelo Gómez, Jaime de Hoyos
Color
81 min.

Roadracers (1994)
Production: Lou Arkoff, Amy Grauman Danziger, Debra Hill
Direction: Robert Rodriguez
Writers: Robert Rodriguez and Tommy Nix
Cinematography: Roberto Schaefer
Editing: Robert Rodriguez
Cast: David Arquette, John Hawkes, Salma Hayek, Jason Wiles, William Sadler
Color
95 min.

Desperado (1995)
Production: Elizabeth Avellán, Bill Borden, Carlos Gallardo, Robert Rodriguez
Direction: Robert Rodriguez
Writer: Robert Rodriguez
Cinematography: Guillermo Navarro
Editing: Robert Rodriguez
Cast: Antonio Banderas, Salma Hayek, Joaquim de Almeida, Cheech Marin, Steve
   Buscemi
Color
106 min.

"The Misbehavers" (in *Four Rooms*) (1995)
Production: Lawrence Bender, Paul Hellerman, Scott Lambert, Alexandre Rockwell,
   Quentin Tarantino, Heidi Vogel
Direction: Robert Rodriguez
Writer: Robert Rodriguez
Cinematography: Rodrigo García, Guillermo Navarro, Phil Parmet, Andrzej Sekula

Editing: Margaret Goodspeed, Elena Maganini, Sally Menke, Robert Rodriguez
Cast: Tim Roth, Antonio Banderas, Tamlyn Tomita, Danny Verduzco, Lana McKissack
Color
102 min.

From Dusk till Dawn (1996)
Production: Elizabeth Avellán, Lawrence Bender, John Esposito, Paul Hellerman, Robert Kurtzman, Gianni Nunnari, Robert Rodriguez, Quentin Tarantino, Meir Teper
Direction: Robert Rodriguez
Writers: Robert Kurtzman (story) and Quentin Tarantino (screenplay)
Cinematography: Guillermo Navarro
Editing: Robert Rodriguez
Cast: Harvey Keitel, George Clooney, Juliette Lewis, Quentin Tarantino, Cheech Marin, Salma Hayek
Color
108 min.

The Faculty (1998)
Production: Elizabeth Avellán, Bill Scott, Tamara Smith, Bob Weinstein, Harvey Weinstein, Robert Rodriguez
Direction: Robert Rodriguez
Writers: David Wechter (story), Bruce Kimmel (story), and Kevin Williamson (screenplay)
Cinematography: Enrique Chediak
Editing: Robert Rodriguez
Cast: Jordana Brewster, Clea DuVall, Laura Harris, Elijah Wood, Joshua Hartnett, Famke Janssen, Salma Hayek, Jon Stewart
Color
104 min.

Spy Kids (2001)
Production: Elizabeth Avellán, Cary Granat, Robert Rodriguez, Bill Scott, Tamara Smith, Bob Weinstein, Harvey Weinstein
Direction: Robert Rodriguez
Writer: Robert Rodriguez
Cinematography: Guillermo Navarro
Editing: Robert Rodriguez
Cast: Alexa Vega, Daryl Sabara, Antonio Banderas, Carla Gugino, Cheech Marin, Danny Trejo
Color
88 min.

Spy Kids 2: Island of Lost Dreams (2002)
Production: Elizabeth Avellán, Robert Rodriguez, Bill Scott, Bob Weinstein, Harvey
    Weinstein
Direction: Robert Rodriguez
Writer: Robert Rodriguez
Cinematography: Robert Rodriguez
Editing: Robert Rodriguez
Cast: Alexa Vega, Daryl Sabara, Antonio Banderas, Steve Buscemi, Carla Gugino,
    Ricardo Montalbán, Bill Paxton
Color
96 min.

Spy Kids 3-D: Game Over (2003)
Production: Elizabeth Avellán, Robert Rodriguez, Bill Scott, Bob Weinstein, Harvey
    Weinstein
Direction: Robert Rodriguez
Writer: Robert Rodriguez (script)
Cinematography: Robert Rodriguez
Editing: Robert Rodriguez
Cast: Daryl Sabara, Alexa Vega, Antonio Banderas, Sylvester Stallone, Salma Hayek
Color
82 min.

Once Upon a Time in Mexico (2003)
Production: Elizabeth Avellán, Carlos Gallardo, Sue Jett, Tony Mark, Robert Rodriguez,
    Luz María Rojas
Direction: Robert Rodriguez
Writer: Robert Rodriguez
Cinematography: Robert Rodriguez
Editing: Robert Rodriguez
Cast: Antonio Banderas, Salma Hayek, Johnny Depp, Mickey Rourke, Eva Mendes,
    Cheech Marin, Danny Trejo
Color
102 min.

Sin City (2005)
Production: Elizabeth Avellán, Bill Scott, Bob Weinstein, Harvey Weinstein
Direction: Frank Miller, Robert Rodriguez
Writer: Frank Miller (graphic novels)
Cinematography: Robert Rodriguez
Editing: Robert Rodriguez
Cast: Mickey Rourke, Clive Owen, Bruce Willis, Jessica Alba, Rosario Dawson, Benicio
    del Toro, Elijah Wood

Color
124 min.

The Adventures of Sharkboy and Lavagirl in 3-D (2005)
Production: Elizabeth Avellán, Bill Scott, Bob Weinstein, Harvey Weinstein
Direction: Robert Rodriguez
Writers: Robert Rodriguez, Marcel Rodriguez, and Racer Rodriguez (story)
Cinematography: Robert Rodriguez
Editing: Robert Rodriguez
Cast: Cayden Boyd, George Lopez, Kristin Davis, David Arquette, Taylor Lautner,
Color
93 min.

Planet Terror (2007)
Production: Robert Rodriguez, Quentin Tarantino, Elizabeth Avellán
Direction: Robert Rodriguez
Writer: Robert Rodriguez
Cinematography: Robert Rodriguez
Editing: Ethan Maniquis, Robert Rodriguez
Cast: Rose McGowan, Freddy Rodriguez, Josh Brolin, Bruce Willis, Naveen Andrews
Color
106 min.

Shorts (2009)
Production: Robert Rodriguez, Elizabeth Avellán
Direction: Robert Rodriguez
Story: Robert Rodriguez and Alvaro Rodriguez
Cinematography: Robert Rodriguez
Editing: Ethan Maniquis, Robert Rodriguez
Cast: Jimmy Bennett, James Spader, Kat Dennings, William H. Macy, Rebel Rodriguez
Color
89 min.

Predators (2010)
Production: Robert Rodriguez, Elizabeth Avellán, John Davis
Direction: Nimród Antal
Writers: Alex Litvak, Michael Finch, Jim Thomas, John Thomas
Cinematography: Gyula Pados
Editing: Dan Zimmerman
Cast: Adrien Brody, Topher Grace, Alice Braga, Laurence Fishburne, Danny Trejo
Color
107 min

Machete (2010)
Production: Ashok Amritraj, Elizabeth Avellán, Alan Bernon, Ed Borgerding, Alastair Burlingham, Dominic Cancilla, Jerry Fruchtman, Peter Fruchtman, Jack Gilardi Jr., etc.
Direction: Ethan Maniquis, Robert Rodriguez
Writers: Robert Rodriguez and Alvaro Rodriguez
Cinematography: Jimmy Lindsey
Editing: Rebecca Rodriguez, Robert Rodriguez
Cast: Danny Trejo, Michelle Rodriguez, Robert De Niro, Jessica Alba, Steven Seagal, Lindsay Lohan, Don Johnson, Cheech Marin
Color
105 min.

The Black Mamba (2011)
Production: Erin Goodsell, Ben Grylewicz, Donna Portaro
Direction: Robert Rodriguez
Writer: Robert Rodriguez
Cinematography: Mauro Fiore
Editing: Angus Wall
Cast: Kobe Bryant, Bruce Willis, Kanye West, Robert Rodriguez
Color
6 min.

Spy Kids 4D: All the Time in the World (2011)
Production: Elizabeth Avellán, George Huang, Tom Proper, Rebecca Rodriguez, Robert Rodriguez, Bob Weinstein, Harvey Weinstein
Direction: Robert Rodriguez
Writer: Robert Rodriguez (screenplay)
Cinematography: Jimmy Lindsey, Robert Rodriguez
Editing: Dan Zimmerman
Cast: Jessica Alba, Jeremy Piven, Joel McHale, Ricky Gervais, Rowan Blanchard, Mason Cook
Color
89 min.

Machete Kills (2013)
Production: Douglas Aarniokoski, Sergei Bespalov, Terry Douglas, Sam Englebardt, William D. Johnson, Aaron Kaufman, Paris Kasidokostas Latsis, Mark C. Manuel, Iliana Nikolic, Alexander Rodnyansky, Robert Rodriguez, Rick Schwartz, Boris Teterev
Direction: Robert Rodriguez
Writers: Marcel Rodriguez (story), Robert Rodriguez (story), and Kyle Ward (screenplay)
Cinematography: Robert Rodriguez

Editing: Robert Rodriguez
Cast: Danny Trejo, Michelle Rodriguez, Jessica Alba, Amber Heard, Carlos Estévez
(Charlie Sheen), Cuba Gooding Jr., Demián Bichir, Mel Gibson, Lady Gaga, Sofía
Vergara
Color
108 min.

Sin City: A Dame to Kill For (2014)
Production: Sergei Bespalov, Aaron Kaufman, Stephen L'Heureux, Robert Rodriguez
Direction: Robert Rodriguez and Frank Miller
Writers: Frank Miller (graphic novels and screenplay), William Monahan (screenplay),
and Robert Rodriguez (screenplay)
Cinematography: Robert Rodriguez
Editing: Robert Rodriguez
Cast: Joseph Gordon-Levitt, Bruce Willis, Josh Brolin, Jessica Alba, Alexa Vega, Mickey
Rourke, Juno Temple
Color
220 min.

Works Cited

Aldama, Frederick Luis, ed. *Critical Approaches to the Films of Robert Rodriguez*. Austin: U of Texas P. Forthcoming.

————, ed. *Latinos and Narrative Media: Participation and Portrayal*. New York: Palgrave Macmillan, 2013.

————. *Mex-Ciné: Mexican Filmmaking, Production, and Consumption in the Twenty-first Century*. Ann Arbor: U of Michigan P, 2013.

Allina, John. "Triplets in Sin: Robert Rodriguez Multiplies *Sin City*'s Film Score." *Sight & Sound* 15.1 (June 2005): 16–18.

Anders, Allison, Alexandre Rockwell, Robert Rodriguez, and Quentin Tarantino. *Four Rooms: Four Friends Telling Four Stories Making One Film*. Los Angeles: Miramax, 1995.

Anderson, Emily R. "*Sin City*, Style, and the Status of Noir." *Critical Approaches to the Films of Robert Rodriguez*. Ed. Frederick Luis Aldama. Austin: U of Texas P. Forthcoming.

Ashcraft, Brian. "The Man Who Shot *Sin City*." *Wired* 13.4 (April 2005) http://www.wired.com/wired/archive/13.04/sincity.html.

Avila, Alex. "25 Most Powerful Hispanics in Hollywood." *Hispanic* 9.4 (April 1996): 20.

Beltrán, Mary C. *Latina/o Stars in U.S. Eyes: The Making and Meanings of Film and TV Stardom*. Chicago: U of Illinois P, 2009.

Bordwell, David. *Narration in the Fiction Film*. Madison: U of Wisconsin P, 1985.

Brecht, Bertolt. *Brecht on Theatre: The Development of an Aesthetic*. Edited and trans. John Willett. New York: Hill and Wang, 1964.

Brown, Jeffrey A. *Dangerous Curves: Action Heroines, Gender, Fetishism, and Popular Culture*. Jackson: UP of Mississippi, 2011.

Buscombe, Edward. "Border Control." *Sight & Sound* 13.10 (October 2003): 22–24.

Cagin, Seth, and Philip Dray. *Hollywood Films of the Seventies: Sex, Drugs, Violence, Rock 'n' Roll & Politics*. New York: Harper & Row, 1984.

Canemaker, John. *Tex Avery: The MGM Years, 1942–1955*. Atlanta: Turner Publishing Inc., 1996.

Chivers, Sally, and Nicole Markotic, eds. *The Problem Body: Projecting Disability in Film.* Columbus: Ohio State UP, 2010.

Corliss, Richard. "Few Bucks, Very Big Bang." *Time* 141.10 (8 Mar. 1993). http://www .time.com/time/magazine/article/0,9171,977898,00.html.

Corman, Roger. *How I Made a Hundred Movies in Hollywood and Never Lost a Dime.* New York: Random House, 1990.

"Did Politics Kill 'Machete' at the Box Office?" http://whatwouldtotowatch.com/2010 /09/13/politics-kill-machetes-box-office/.

Donahue, James J. "Social Minds in the Cinema: The Development of *El Mariachi*." *Critical Approaches to the Films of Robert Rodriguez.* Ed. Frederick Luis Aldama. Austin: U of Texas P. Forthcoming.

Doyle, Audrey. "Spying in Stereo." *Computer Graphics World* 26.8 (August 2003): 24.

Ebert, Roger. "*Spy Kids.*" (Review). http://www.rogerebert.com/reviews/spy-kids-2001.

Eighan, Erin. "*Sin City*, Hybrid Media, and a Cognitive Narratology of Multimodality." *Critical Approaches to the Films of Robert Rodriguez.* Ed. Frederick Luis Aldama. Austin: U of Texas P. Forthcoming.

Engber, Daniel. "Why Not Quit the Directors Guild? What Robert Rodriguez Can and Can't Do." *Slate.* http://www.slate.com/articles/news_and_politics/explainer /2005/04/why_not_quit_the_directors_guild.html.

Espinoza, Galina. "Better to Bring Latinos into TV's Mainstream." *USA Today*, 23 Mar. 2012, News Section: 11a.

Fojas, Camilla. *Border Bandits: Hollywood on the Southern Frontier.* Austin: U of Texas P, 2008.

Frayling, Christopher. *Spaghetti Westerns: Cowboys and Europeans from Karl May to Sergio Leone.* New York: Palgrave Macmillan, 2006.

Fregoso, Rosa-Linda. *The Bronze Screen: Chicana and Chicano Film Culture.* Minneapolis: U of Minnesota P, 1993.

Fridlund, Bert. *The Spaghetti Western: A Thematic Analysis.* Jefferson, NC: McFarland, 2006.

García, Enrique. "*Planet Terror* Redux: Miscegenation and Family Apocalypse." *Critical Approaches to the Films of Robert Rodriguez.* Ed. Frederick Luis Aldama. Austin: U of Texas P. Forthcoming.

Gardner, Jared. *Projections: Comics and the History of Twenty-First-Century Storytelling.* Stanford: Stanford UP, 2012.

Garson, Charlotte. "Mexploitation." *Cahiers du Cinema* 662 (December 2010): 43.

González, Christopher. "Intertextploitation and Post Post-Latinidad in *Planet Terror.*" *Critical Approaches to the Films of Robert Rodriguez.* Ed. Frederick Luis Aldama. Austin: U of Texas P. Forthcoming.

———, ed. *The Films of Robert Rodriguez. Post Script: Essays in Film and the Humanities.* Special issue. Forthcoming.

Grodal, Torben. "Pain, Sadness, Aggression, and Joy: An Evolutionary Approach to Film Emotions." *Projections* 1.1 (Summer 2007): 91–107.

Hale, Mike. "Very Busy Mom Faces a Bigger Mission." *New York Times* 19 Aug. 2011: C6.

Heide, Markus. "The History of Chicano Film: Hybridity and Intercultural Exchanges as Representational Practices." *Hybrid Americas: Contacts, Contrasts, and Confluences in New World Literatures and Cultures*. Eds. Josef Raab and Martin Butler. Berlin, Germany: Verlag, 2008. 249–264.

Helyer, Ruth. "Parodied to Death: The Postmodern Gothic of American Psycho." *MFS Modern Fiction Studies* 46.3 (Fall 2000): 725–746.

Hogan, Patrick Colm. "Painterly Cinema: Three Minutes of *Sin City*." *Critical Approaches to the Films of Robert Rodriguez*. Ed. Frederick Luis Aldama. Austin: U of Texas P. Forthcoming.

————. *The Mind and Its Stories: Narrative Universals and Human Emotion*. Cambridge, UK: Cambridge UP, 2003.

Hughes, Howard. *Upon a Time in the Italian West: A Filmgoers' Guide to Spaghetti Westerns*. London: I. B. Taurus, 2005.

Ingle, Zachary, ed. *Robert Rodriguez: Interviews*. Jackson: UP of Mississippi, 2012.

————. "The Border Crossed Us: *Machete* and the Latino Threat Narrative." *Critical Approaches to the Films of Robert Rodriguez*. Ed. Frederick Luis Aldama. Austin: U of Texas P. Forthcoming.

Irwin, Mark. "Pulp & the Pulpit: The Films of Quentin Tarantino and Robert Rodriguez." *Literature & Theology* 12.1 (March 1998): 70–81.

Jones, Kimberley. "*Spy Kids 3-D: Game Over*." *Austin Chronicle* 25 July 2003. http://www.austinchronicle.com/calendar/film/2003-07-25/169586/.

Keller, Gary, ed. *Chicano Cinema: Research, Reviews, and Resources*. Binghamton, NY: Bilingual Review P, 1985.

Kim, Sue J. "From *El Mariachi* Till *Spy Kids*?: A Cognitive Approach." In *Latinos and Narrative Media: Participation and Portrayal*. Ed. Frederick Luis Aldama. New York: Palgrave Macmillan, 2013. 195–210.

King, Geoff. *American Independent Cinema*. Bloomington: IN. Indiana UP, 2005.

Macor, Alison. *Chainsaws, Slackers, and Spy Kids*. Austin: U of Texas P, 2010.

Martinez, Javier A. "Planet Terror (Review)." *Science Fiction Film and Television* 3.2 (Autumn 2010): 331–335.

Marvis, Mary J. *Robert Rodriguez*. Childs, MD: Mitchell Lane, 1998.

McGee, Patrick. *From Shane to Kill Bill: Rethinking the Western*. Malden, MA: Blackwell, 2007.

McGinn, Colin. *The Power of Movies*. New York: Random House, 2005.

McKernan, Brian, and Bob Zahn. "A Digital Desperado." *Robert Rodriguez: Interviews*. Ed. Zachary Ingle. Jackson: UP of Mississippi, 2012. 75–77.

McRoy, Jay. "'The Kids of Today Should Defend Themselves Against the '70s': Simulating Auras and Marketing Nostalgia in Robert Rodriguez and Quentin Tarantino's *Grindhouse*." *American Horror Film: The Genre at the Turn of the Millennium*. Ed. Steffen Hantke. Jackson: UP of Mississippi, 2010. 221–234.

Migneco, Fabio. *Il cinema di Robert Rodriguez*. Piombino, Livorno: Edizioni il Foglio, 2009.

Miller, Frank, and Robert Rodriguez. *Frank Miller's Sin City: The Making of the Movie*. Austin: Troublemaker P, 2005.

Mitchell, Elvis. "Espionage Is the Family Business, Even in a Fun Factory." *New York Times*, 30 Mar. 2001: 12.

Mize, Ronald L., and Grace Peña Delgado. *Latino Immigrants in the United States*. Cambridge, UK: Polity, 2012.

Molina-Guzmán, Isabel. *Dangerous Curves: Latina Bodies in the Media*. New York: New York University Press, 2010.

Newitz, Annalee. *Pretend We're Dead: Capitalist Monsters in American Pop Culture*. Durham: Duke UP, 2006.

———. "What Makes Things Cheesy?" *Social Text* 63.2 (Summer 2000): 59–82.

Newman, Kim. "Once Upon a Time in Mexico." *Sight & Sound* 13.11 (2003): 58–59.

———. "Sin City." *Sight & Sound* 15.6 (2005): 72–73.

Noriega, Chon A., ed. *Chicanos and Film: Essays on Chicano Representation and Resistance*. New York: Garland P, 1992.

———. *Shot in America: Television, the State, and the Rise of Chicano Cinema*. Minneapolis: U of Minnesota P, 2000.

Noriega, Chon, and Ana López, eds. *The Ethnic Eye: Latino Media Arts*. Minneapolis: U of Minnesota P, 1996.

Pierson, John. *Spike, Mike, Slackers & Dykes: A Guided Tour Across a Decade of American Independent Cinema*. New York: Miramax Books/Hyperion, 1995.

Pinsker, Beth. "Filmmakers in the Fast Lane." *Entertainment Weekly* 23 June 1995, Issue 280.

Place-Verghnes, Floriane. *Tex Avery: A Unique Legacy (1942–1955)*. Eastleigh, UK: John Libbey Publishing, 2006.

Ramírez Berg, Charles. "Ethnic Ingenuity and Mainstream Cinema: Robert Rodriguez's Bedhead (1990) and El Mariachi (1993)." *The Ethnic Eye: Latino Media Arts*. Eds. Chon Noriega and Ana López. Minneapolis: U of Minnesota P, 1996. 107–128.

———. *Latino Images in Film: Stereotypes, Subversion, Resistance*. Austin: U of Texas P, 2002.

Renga, Dana. "Pastapocalypse! End Times in Italian Trash Cinema." *The Italianist* 31 (2011): 243–257.

Rizov, Vadim. "Machete." *Sight & Sound* 20.12 (Dec. 2010): 70.

Rodriguez, Álvaro. "Post-production in Robert Rodriguez's 'Post-post Latinidad': An Afterword." In *Critical Approaches to the Films of Robert Rodriguez*. Ed. Frederick Luis Aldama. Austin: U of Texas P. Forthcoming.

Rodriguez, Robert. *Rebel Without a Crew, or, How a 24-Year-Old Filmmaker with $7,000 Became a Hollywood Player*. New York: Dutton, 1995.

Rodriguez, Robert, Aaron Kaufman, and Stuart Sayger. *Machete #0*. San Diego: IDW Publishing, September 2010.

Rodriguez, Robert, and Frank Miller. *Frank Miller's Sin City: The Making of the Movie*. Austin: Troublemaker P, 2005.

Rodriguez, Robert, Chris Roberson, and Alex Toader. *Sharkboy and Lavagirl Adventures: Book 1*. Austin: Troublemaker P, 2005.

Rodriguez, Robert, Chris Roberson, and Alex Toader. *Sharkboy and Lavagirl Adventures: Book 2*. Austin: Troublemaker P, 2005.

Rodriguez, Robert, and Racer Max Rodriguez. *The Adventures of Sharkboy and Lavagirl: The Movie Storybook*. Austin: TroubleMaker P, 2005.

Rodriguez, Robert, and Quentin Tarantino. *Grindhouse: The Sleaze-Filled Saga of an Exploitation Double Feature*. New York: Weinstein Books, 2007.

Savlov, Marc. "Violent Ends Fifteen Years after First Inception, 'Machete' Hacks Its Way into Theatres." *Austin Chronicle* 30 Sept. 2010. http://www.austinchronicle.com/screens/2010-09-03/1077219/.

Serrato, Phillip. "You've Come a Long Way, Booger Breath: Juni Cortez Grows Up in Robert Rodriguez's *Spy Kids* Films." *Critical Approaches to the Films of Robert Rodriguez*. Ed. Frederick Luis Aldama. Austin: U of Texas P. Forthcoming.

Sipos, Thomas M. *Horror Film Aesthetics: Creating the Visual Language of Fear*. Jefferson, NC: McFarland, 2010.

Stevenson, Jack. "Grindhouse and Beyond." *From the Arthouse to the Grindhouse: Highbrow and Lowbrow Transgression in Cinema's First Century*. Eds. John Cline and Robert G. Weiner. Plymouth, UK: Scarecrow P, 2010. 129–152.

Tauber, Michelle, and Gabrielle Cosgriff. "Who's the Grown-Up?" *People* 60.5 (4 Aug. 2003).

Torres, Hector A. "Chicano Doppelganger: Robert Rodriguez's First Remake and Secondary Revision." *Aztlán* 26.1 (2001): 159–171.

Travers, Peter. "El Mariachi and the Sundance Kid." *Rolling Stone* 18 Mar. 1993, 49.

———. "*Grindhouse*" (Review). *Rolling Stone* 3 April 2007.

———. "On the Move with Robert Rodriguez." *Rolling Stone* 18 Mar. 1993, 47.

Wilson, Vicky. "Faster Cooler Smarter Taller." *Sight & Sound* 12 (2003): 52–53.

Wood, Jason. *100 American Independent Films*. London: BFI, 2004.

Index

Page numbers in italics indicate figures.